WAYS OF INDIAN WISDOM

WAYS
OF
INDIAN WISDOM

Stories Retold
by
Teresa VanEtten

Sunstone Press
Santa Fe, New Mexico

To Musa, who taught me how to accept life and listen.
Thank you, Nicole and Claire, for waiting.

First Edition, Second Printing

Printed in the United States of America

Library of Congress Cataloging in Publication Data:

VanEtten, Teresa, 1951-
    Ways of Indian Wisdom.

        Contents: Introduction -- The grandson's wisdom --
Queen of the white corn -- |etc.|
        1. Pueblo Indians--Legends. 2. Indians of
North America--Southwest, New--Legends. I. Title.
E99.P9V37   1987   813'.54   86-5924
ISBN 0-86534-090-0

Published in 1990 by SUNSTONE PRESS
                Post Office Box 2321
                Santa Fe, NM 87504-2321, USA

CONTENTS

INTRODUCTION

Passages of people, placed on personal paths, press to mind. Their presence, ever so important, brings tears to my eyes. Tales of people not to be forgotten, but to be remembered, for the feeling behind the tales brings strength to the listener.

Grandfather, a name of respect to a wise one who considered himself indebted to my father for saving his life, wanted to return the favor by teaching me basketweaving and storytelling. We became fast friends with emotional responsibilities to each other.

The Pueblo now is separate from most of my family. The Mercantile they once owned burned to the ground on a hot July morning. My parents live far to the south, my brothers are married and live their own lives in other towns. I am now living in a college town miles from the people I grew up with and miss.

Strange as it may seem, I thought all the world was like the Pueblo. The places on the maps were smaller or larger Pueblos, people like those I knew. How peculiar to envision people and places that I could not identify as someone or something I already had worked so hard to know. All people that I have known and met do have one thing uniquely their own — their stories. Stories unite all of these people, sacred soulful stories that are magical. The wisdom of the ways is to be held in harmony as a sacred song, the magic savored as it enters your soul.

"Believing what you are told in terms of words can turn your mind cold. Believing what you are told in terms of feelings can enrich your being. Here, hold these." Long stemmed willows with white slashes were handed to me. "Stories are to be remembered for the way they make you feel, not for the actual wording. How many do we have?"

"We have four piles as tall as my knee." My words were small compared to the roaring river. "Grandfather, when will you teach me what the river sings?"

"The river sings to those who will listen. Only those who listen can understand the song of time. Today, you are going to help me with my basketweaving." Grandfather slipped his sharp knife into his belt. "You are good with your hands, they hold feeling that should be put into beauty. Here, you carry these, I will take the rest to the truck."

The green willows were heavy. Once they were dried, they were lifeless and light. I carried my bunch of willow to the dirty truck. Mud had decorated the sides and most of the windows. Grandfather pulled me up onto the back of the flatbed. "You sit here and hold them down. The bumpy road home will knock them off if you don't hold them." I did as I was told.

The wind blew through my long hair. The willows bounced, struggling for freedom, not knowing that their capture would be beautiful. The adobe home was cold when we arrived. The fire warmed Grandfather's hands as they worked twisting the soaked willow that was picked yesterday. The wrinkled hands moved with great agility. My hands were busy stripping off what little bark there was on the green willow.

"You are a quiet one, Nee-nee," Grandfather smiled. "What is it you want to know about the river? Do you want to know the stories it tells?" The willows dripped on the mud floor. "Do you want to know about the stories that the river told me when I was younger?"

He wrapped the willows one over the other. They stopped being long pieces of wood and turned into decorative scalloped lace work. "When I was younger, the river was less complicated. It rolled down from the mountains with stories of the times that had come before."

His brown eyes widened. I knew better than to speak. He would say what he wanted to say. The willow pile grew smaller and smaller. His voice deepened and the story began.

1

GRANDSON'S WISDOM

Seasons of time grow old. The younger seasons would care for the older seasons and learn their knowledge. Pueblos would shelter their old wise ones with great pride. However, the seasons change and with the change in seasons comes the change in caring. Each began to care more for their own weather than for the weather of the old wise ones.

A young man, Tsay-Whan T'a, a basketmaker, found the weather cold and indifferent. He would not spend this winter alone, trying to warm himself in a bedroll that would wind around him leaving his legs to the cold night air. Tsay-Whan T'a asked Than Bee to be his woman and keep him warm through the time of the bare trees and the thick snows. She agreed, with her parents' consent, and they were married before the summer became hot. She was older, plumper, and a better cook than Tsay-Whan T'a or his father Agoyo P'in.

Agoyo P'in watched Tsay-Whan T'a move his wife into the mud home. Agoyo P'in helped in the garden at harvest for Tsay-Whan T'a slept later now. Agoyo P'in held great strength in his mind and his hands. He had been gifted with the ability to cure sick animals. Cornmeal, saps, smelly creams, clean cloths, chants that calmed the animal in the night, brought about a cure. A coyote call from across the canyon would wake him in the night. The repetition of the call told him how far away the animal in need of care was.

On a night of the even summer wind, there came such a call. Agoyo P'in dressed, pulling on his moccasins at the door. His return answer was that of a hawk's mating call. He lifted his medicine bag off the chair. Pulling it firmly around his neck he would run with the wind, his feet not touching the sandy dirt, and he would be there.

His fingers touching the small baby goat told him of the problem. Agoyo P'in pulled out a feather and with his sharp knife cut the feather from the strong stem making a straw with a sharp point. He inserted this into the goat's throat drawing no blood, blowing down the feather stem the goat started to breathe easily without pain. Agoyo P'in wrapped the goat in the wet cloth the owner had brought him. "This one is getting into the thick weed that blocks the throat. You should keep him away from the flatland cactus and weeds." The owner of the goat gave Agoyo P'in a roll of meat jerky.

Agoyo P'in pulled his medicine bag back around his neck, patted the goat, and with a nod started home. His long white hair flowed out behind him only to fall down on his back with the stillness of his spirit. Agoyo P'in returned home.

This was his home of mud that he had built long ago for his woman and son. His woman had the illness. She was restless, angry, filled with remorse all the time. She spat blood and died leaving him with a young son, a son who spoke little and wove baskets a lot. A boy who grew into a man and brought a woman into his home, a woman who made him feel like an outcast.

The fall winds blew gently at first, almost in warning of what was to come. The reds and golds were not yet fully upon the trees and brush of the mountains. The winds gained in strength, blowing in with them the change of dark lush greens to fading browns which illuminated the canyons with yellows that were lit each night by the chilling air.

Than Bee kept the fires burning in the early dark of winter. She became restless in the night for her season of child bearing was coming. She wanted Agoyo P'in out of her home and into a place of his own. Than Bee told her husband that she could no longer live with the old Agoyo P'in or the cries of the hawk in the middle of the night.

Tsay-Whan T'a gathered up his knife and leather thongs; he would let the willows guide him. He came to a spring he had not seen before. The willows were high and thin. They cut easily with his sharp knife. The view of the Pueblo beyond was what gave him his answer. The Pueblo was within a good five minute run. The tall trees would shelter this area from the high winds of fall and spring. The calls in the night bounced off the high gorge wall behind where the spring started. Tsay-Whan T'a put his willow down. He cleared the thick sandy-clay soil away pouring water on what remained. This made a hard floor. He then took the willows he had cut and wove them together to make a thick cedar mat. He made four of these mats, each in turn strapped to the cedar trees. They were firmly held, and thick enough to keep in the warmth of the fire.

Tsay-Whan T'a then cut smaller branches of cedar and wrapped the willow around them, binding them together as a roof. The roof was then covered with mud, packed with pinon needles and left to dry in the sun. Tsay-Whan T'a gathered dry wood making a pile of firewood outside the sliding mat that would be used for the door. The purple hue of evening fell across the land. It was done, it was time for him to go home and tell of his decision. Tsay-Whan T'a ran as an elk loping across the plains. His mind was made up, but his heart was unsure. He ate his evening meal in silence watching his father's sunburnt face. The wrinkles of time shone proudly on the old man's brow. Eyes watched eyes with caution. Agoyo P'in wiped his hands for he was finished with his meal. The two men nodded in agreement and walked outside.

The sky was lit with many stars. Tsay-Whan T'a broke the crisp silence of the night, "Father, you are the one they call Star Mountain at night, is that not so?"

"Tsay-Whan T'a, you have known that for a long time. What is heavy in your mind is also heavy in mine. Is it time for my life to be elsewhere?"

"Yes, I have built you a lean-to not far from the farming lands. You will be near the spring and have an easy walk to any animal that may need your care." Tsay-Whan T'a turned, leaving his father alone outside the home that once was his.

The next morning, Agoyo P'in rolled his belongings into his bedroll. The smell of the pinon burning in the kitchen fire was a smell he would always remember.

"Father, are you ready?" Tsay-Whan T'a was anxious to be finished with this move. Perhaps now he could lead his own life without his father watching him, judging him without words.

Agoyo P'in dropped his belongings into the lean-to. "This is strong, you have built it well. How long do you think that I must stay here? The winter will be long and the winds cold."

Tsay-Whan T'a watched his father's hands stroke the lean-to's walls. The open side was shielded. "The time for you to return will be told to us. Now we must wait."

Agoyo P'in set up his things in his new home.

Tsay Whan T'a lay close to his woman in the warm bedroll. He placed his hand on his woman's belly feeling his baby move. In the night's stillness came the sound of a coyote calling out, then in answer the hawk. Tsay-Whan T'a knew his family was safe.

Spring broke forth in song with the birth of a boy. The little baby was called Oekuu Tsaa after a small white turtle fetish from his kuliohatsiper. The boy grew strong and big with an open curiosity.

Oekuu Tsaa turned five years old. The thick grasses of summer mixed with the cool winds of fall once more. Oekuu Tsaa no longer wanted to run with his friends. He wanted to learn of what lay further out of the Pueblo. Oekuu Tsaa watched the hawks move in pairs across the sky. One would turn, dive out of sight and then reappear with a lizard or snake in its mouth. Oekuu Tsaa watched the snakes sun on the hot rocks of the plains. Then when a moving shadow fell across the ground they would magically disappear. Oekuu Tsaa followed the hawks wanting to learn of their way. On such an adventure an old female hawk called out to the boy. She dove down into the grass flapping her wings, flying up within his sight, then falling into the grass. She led him to a spring. The water was clear trickling in song. Oekuu Tsaa listened yet further and heard the song of an elder floating through the willow. The female hawk flapped her way to an old man sitting by a lean-to. The Elder lifted up the old female hawk and stroked her feathers.

"You need attention, do you?" He stroked her head feathers letting her peck softly at his arm.

Oekuu Tsaa studied the old man. The man turned his head as a hawk would, with a jerk, then stillness. A song flowed from the Elder's chapped lips. Oekuu Tsaa moved closer to the old man.

The old man frowned, stopping his song, "The song is of my friend the hawk; are you a hawk?"

"I am a white turtle. My name is Oekuu Tsaa."

The old man smiled. He clapped his hands together, "I know who you are. You are the son of Tsay-Whan T'a, who is my son."

"That is right, Grandfather, but why don't you live with us? Why do you live here in a lean-to at the edge of a spring?"

Agoyo P'in studied the boy's bright eyes. They were dark brown with the line of knowledge outlining his eyelashes. "I live here for there is no room in your home for this old one."

Oekuu Tsaa touched the wrinkled, calloused hands. "You are cold. Do you have a blanket?"

Agoyo P'in lowered his eyes. "No, I have had food and still do, but I do not have a blanket."

Oekuu Tsaa heard the hawks cry out over the gorge. "I will get you a blanket. I will be back before the sun sets." The boy ran through the grass plains and hurried into his home.

Tsay-Whan T'a caught his son as he ran through the home. "Where are you going my fast one?"

The boy pulled loose. "I am going to get my blanket and with a knife I will cut it into two parts of the same size."

Tsay-Whan T'a let go of his squirming son. "Why do you want to cut a blanket your mother has worked so hard to weave? Where would you go with it?"

Oekuu Tsaa looked proudly at his father. "I will give one part of the blanket to the old wise one who lives by the spring with the tall willow, for he is your father. He is cold at night with only food but no blanket. I must take it to him before the sun sets."

Tsay-Whan T'a studied his son's face. "What will you do with the other half of the blanket?"

Oekuu Tsaa smiled, "I will save it and when you live in the lean-to by the spring and are old I will give it to you."

Reds and browns highlighted the river. The old female hawk turned away from her partner in the sky and dove down for the evening hunt.

The stripped willows lay limp on the floor. Grandfather was busy in thought and weaving. I knew better than to interrupt him. I gathered up the stripped bark. It would go next door to the widow. She uses the bark on her pots. No one has seen her use it nor do they know exactly what she does with it, but Grandfather says she polishes the unfired pots with the bark. I take it to her.

Her wraps are many, they keep her warm wrapped around her shoulders and middle. "Nee-nee, thank you for the bark. It has been many days since I have seen you. What have you been doing in town?"

She asks if I would like some hot tea. This is our routine, I enjoy her stories and she enjoys my company. Grandfather feels that it is important to listen. She tells me of her son.

"He must live far away for he does not belong here. He was born here, his people are here, his home is here, but he is not at peace here. He must grow like a tree in the environment that will keep him alive." A long orange cat walked into the room. He sniffed my legs, meowed and jumped into the widow's lap. The cat purred in her lap. "This story is about a woman. You will know of the feelings in this story. This story is very old. Older than I am, older than words. Listen with your soul."

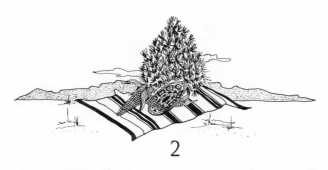

2
QUEEN OF THE WHITE CORN

The stillness in the small room was broken with words. "Push, push, now!" Sweat dripped from the mother's face as she bore down hard. The Pu'fona rubbed the mother's belly. The mother groaned. The Pu'fona pushed the palm of her hand down hard on the belly, "Push, push, the sun is fading, push." The mother heard the words that were screamed at her. She pushed and pushed but the pain was more than she could bear. "Did you walk over a sleeping dog? Did you help your man clean his bows for the hunt?" The mother shook her head no. "The sun is going, the sun is going into the other world!" The Pu'fona pulled open her medicine bag. She pulled out a round fat ear of white corn, then she pulled out a flat branched-out ear of dark blue-black corn. She placed these two ears of corn on either side of the mother's legs. The mother bit down on her lip, blood oozed down her chin. The baby would not come.

The Pu'fona took a wrapped bundle from her medicine bag. She unwrapped it dropping the powder into a gourd of water. The water turned blue. She lifted the gourd of water to the mother's lips. "Drink this, drink quickly. This will save your baby from harm. This will make the baby strong in the ways of wisdom." The mother drank the cool liquid. It relaxed her body. The baby slid out into the hands of the medicine woman. The sky went black. Chanters in the bubinge stopped their chanting and ran for cover in the kivas.

The mother took the baby girl from the medicine woman. The Pu'fona smiled, "Do not fear, the evil ones cannot hurt you or the baby. I am strong in my ways and do not fear them. Let the others hide, you rest and hold your baby. Follow the ritual and all will be well." The medicine woman wrapped the baby in soft furs and placed the little girl at her mother's breast. The baby suckled hungrily. "There now, you rest."

The medicine woman knelt on the ground next to them and began to sing. She took another ear of the dark flat branched-out corn laying it near the baby's head. She picked up the other by the mother's leg and placed it under the mother's arm near the baby. The white corn had fallen away. The Pu'fona lifted the white corn over the baby. The white corn turned dark. The Pu'fona's voice was soft and flowing through the darkness that had taken the sun's light away. Slowly the light came back into the darkness. The sun gained back its strength in the sky and turned the world of darkness back to light.

The father of the baby entered the hut. "How is she? How is the baby?"

The Pu'fona gathered up her belongings. "She is very tired, the baby was not ready to come out of the window into this world of darkness. The baby is fine."

The father noticed the dark ears of corn, "The baby is a girl. That is good." They walked out of the home.

The Pu'fona whispered to the father, "You must watch the baby. Her beauty is great for she has been given a gift beyond compare from the Great-Up-Above-Spirits. The others in the Pueblo will be cautious of her for she was born at the time of the evil ones' entry. I gave your woman and child a specific brew that kept them safe. You must believe in what you feel, not in what you hear." The evil ball of darkness was still in the sky moving away from the sun. The medicine woman, Pu'fona, took her pay of meat, then went back to her home in the mountains.

The father hurried to his sister's home and told her of the birth of his daughter. He was the father of a healthy, beautiful baby girl. His sister did not show emotion at the news. She knew of the powers in the sun, she knew of the evil spirits that could remove fingers and toes replacing them with an evil that was hidden behind beauty.

"You go to the elders and tell them of your child. I will get our younger sister and your woman's sister, we will come for the cleansing." She did not smile or give him any sign of her feelings to help him with his worries. She gathered up her blanket and ran out the door calling out behind to him, "This is not your doing, it is your woman's."

The father told the Elders of his daughter's birth and the pride he felt in his fatherhood. Then he went back home. "Are you awake? My sisters are coming and so is yours. They will do the cleansing ceremony right away."

The mother groaned, "It is too soon, it is not right. We must wait three days. I cannot walk, this is too soon."

The father stroked the baby girl's soft head. "It will be good to do this now. The Elders cannot scold us, this will help the baby bring good fortune to the people." The mother pulled herself up to a sitting position. "Get me water, I must bathe before they come."

The mother washed her body and her hair while the father spoke with the sisters outside. He had built a fire for the cooking of corn and the cleansing of the blankets. The women talked of names for the girl. It was decided that the girl would get her name when she was a year old. That way they would be sure that they had not named an evil spirit.

"The Kaiye names the baby when it is born. That is the way that my people were taught."

The father's sister spoke, "No, the Ko'o will name the child for the time being until we are sure that this one is not bringing destruction to our lives."

"What about you? You are the Ki'i, will you give this little one a name?" The older sister confronted the father's sister.

"Yes, I will name her Khuu Oyegi." The sisters burst out in laughter.

The father felt the anger in him rise. "You will wait for a name. Let us think well of her until she shows us differently."

"It is not sunrise, but the sun has started to shine for a second time this day. We will do the ceremony now rather than wait until tomorrow."

Father went into the home and carried out his woman who held the baby to her breast. The Ki'i (father's sister) took the baby from the mother. She carried the baby to a circle the Kaiye had drawn in the dirt. The Kaiye and the Ko'o swept the circle clean around the Ki'i. The Kaiyo slashed out at the air, cutting up any evil spirits that were trying to enter the soul of the baby. The fire stick was thrown into the fire and burned. The baby started to cry.

They carried the baby into the home. On the floor was a clean bowl of bath water. The water had an oga placed in the bottom of it, it sparkled in the bowl. The Ki'i knelt down with the baby by the bowl of water. The Ki'i had now become the Tsitsayiya, the one who will give the baby her name for life. The father was proud that his sister was courageous enough to do this over the others.

His sister, the Ki'i, now rinsed off the baby, then took up an abalone shell. She filled the shell with the bath water, taking a mouthful of it she breathed hard in and out, then on the third intake of air, she put her mouth to the baby and let the water go from her mouth to the baby's mouth. She did this again only this time she picked up each ear of dark corn and breathed in and out along the sides of them. On her last breath of air she breathed out on the baby's mouth. The other two sisters repeated this same ceremony. The mother sat down leaning against the side of the doorway. Her hands were shaking, her head hurt with the silence of the ceremony and the intensity of emotions mixed with magic.

The Ki'i pulled a small fetish stone from her belt wrap placing it on the baby's belly. The two ears of corn they placed carefully along the sides of the baby's head. Each sister then stood up, bowed to each other and walked out around the weak mother.

The father met them outside with hot stew and bread that he had saved from the last baking day. They thanked him and went on their way giggling and laughing. The father cautiously went into his home. His woman was lying on her side by the baby. "So, they have performed the Kudioaniyima. She will have a better chance."

The mother looked up at him. "A better chance of what?"

The days moved on from the day the sun was hidden behind the evil ball. Mother and father remained by themselves. The people in the Pueblo spoke of the evil child, the child who must be killed, the time of trial by the girl child. When the baby was a year old, the Elders came to their home. They spoke into the night of how the spirits had warned them of an evil child. It was time for mother and father to kill their beautiful baby so that the people could rest with the goodness that they had worked so hard for through the ages of time.

The mother sat nursing her baby. The father sat quietly on the floor of his home. They listened, they heard the words of warning, but in their hearts they knew that the baby was not evil and that she would not bring evil to the people. The people themselves would bring on their own evil.

At last the Elders left them to their own thoughts. The father knelt beside his woman. "What are we to do? They will kill the baby if we don't. They will kill all of us if we do not do what they want."

Mother nodded, "There is a grandmother of yours that lives near the Pueblo to the west of us. We could take this little one to her until after the evil thoughts have gone away. We could tell them that she died unexpectedly." Mother pulled her baby to her, father said nothing.

In the evening before the snows came, father took mother aside. "We will do as you suggested. We will take the baby to Grandmother Anina. She knows the ways of children and she is clever enough to answer questions that need answering for her people. We will go in the morning light."

Mother carried her baby wrapped in a blanket. Father carried the food, clothing and gifts. Anina met them with great joy. She had lived alone for many years, she treasured the baby with great love. Mother and father left the baby feeling good about the situation.

17

The baby girl grew. Grandmother Anina could deny the girl nothing. On the first trip to the Pueblo, people began to talk. Grandmother Anina spoke right up, "She is my granddaughter and I am to raise her." They need not know more.

The girl grew to be five years old. Grandmother Anina decided to call the girl Povi. Povi was quick to learn the ways of planting, harvesting and cooking. Povi tried all of the arts that her Grandmother Anina showed her. Povi was very good at bark paintings.

Fall weather with its greens fading into golden browns brought an illness to Grandmother Anina. Her hands became thick and painful. Grandmother Anina needed help in the mornings to get out of her bedroll. Povi learned how to do a lot of the small things that her Grandmother Anina had done before, but now could not do with the cold stillness creeping into her bones.

Povi asked Grandmother Anina to tell her of the Pueblo and the people where she had come from when she was born. Grandmother Anina told Povi of the sun's pink rays of light that brought her to this place. Grandmother Anina did not tell Povi of her parents nor of the circumstances that led to Povi's life with her. Povi accepted Grandmother Anina as her only living relative and friend. They worked well together and they could share feelings without speaking.

Grandmother Anina decided that it was time to go into the Pueblo and talk with the Medicine Man about her pain. Povi helped her grandmother to the Medicine Man's home. Grandmother asked Povi to play outside. Povi put her little bundle down and played with her corn husk dolls. Some other children came up to her and asked if they could play. She was surprised, "Yes." They were all having great fun when one of the mothers who was baking at a nearby horno saw them.

"Morning Flower, you get away from her." The mother ran over and picked up her little girl. "You stay away from this one here. She is evil. Did you touch her things? You did. Well run and wash your hands with blue cornmeal. Hurry!"

The little girl was carried away from Povi crying, "I like her, I want to play with her." Harsh words followed and the girl disappeared. Other mothers came when they heard the commotion and took their daughters away, too. Povi stood up with tears of anger. She picked up her dolls and ran all the way home.

Grandmother Anina came out of the Medicine Man's home looking for Povi. One of the mothers came over to her, "Your evil one has gone home. Keep her away from us and our children. Do you hear me, you old witch, keep her away!"

Grandmother Anina stared at the mothers around her. Their eyes were filled with anger and fear. She lifted her sack over her back and walked home slowly in pain for fear that Povi too might have felt the hurt.

Grandmother Anina walked into the two-room hut. There on the floor were Povi's dolls. They were all torn up with legs and heads thrown all about the room. Grandmother Anina took a peppermint stick out of her sack and went out into the back. There under the tallest cottonwood tree sat Povi, crying. Grandmother Anina walked softly behind the tree, and stuck the peppermint out around Povi's little trembling body. In a deep voice she said, "The good spirits want you to have this." Povi took the stick and looked behind her, there was no one there. Grandmother Anina had moved quickly behind another tree. Povi wiped her tears and knelt down to find her grandmother. No sooner had she done this when her grandmother fell over on the ground.

Povi ran to her, "Grandmother Anina, are you all right?" The grandmother did not move. Povi listened for her breath. Grandmother Anina was still breathing, but she was sound asleep. The sky had turned dark. Povi looked up at the sky, dark heavy rain clouds were coming closer and closer. Povi looked around for some shelter, there was none except the home, but that was too far for her to carry her grandmother.

"Please, Great-Up-Above-Spirits, help me get my grandmother well. Please do not rain until she is inside. Please help me." Povi wished with all her might. The sky turned very dark and the air stood still. A large gust of wind blew out of nowhere. It lifted Grandmother Anina off the ground, whisked her through the door opening and into the back room. The wind blew a soft breeze past Povi and the bedroll opened. Grandmother Anina was gently lowered onto the bedroll. Povi stood in the room with her hands held out, "Thank you, thank you."

The wind rushed around Povi, tousled her hair and then floated out of the house dropping the door opening blankets behind it. The rain poured down and the thunder rolled across the land. Povi knelt near Grandmother Anina. The dark sky with cold winds penetrated the small mud hut. The storm passed, many days passed. Povi gave her grandmother nourishment, medicine, and kept her warm through the cold winter months.

One spring evening Povi knelt over her Grandmother Anina. "I miss you, I need you to be here with me. Please wake up and be with me." Povi's tears streamed down her face. They fell on her grandmother's eyelids. Grandmother's breathing changed, her eyes blinked, her lips moved.

"Grandmother, I am right here, please speak." Grandmother Anina smiled.

Povi helped her grandmother sit up and drink some broth. Slowly, slowly Grandmother Anina gained her strength back. She noticed a side of Povi she had not remembered. Povi had become very quiet, painting all day without speaking. Grandmother Anina soon felt well enough to go into the Pueblo for some supplies.

They went into the Pueblo in the morning. Povi helped her grandmother order and pack the items that they bought. Povi's face remained hard and cold staring straight ahead as they walked out of the Pueblo. Children came running up to them shouting and pointing, "There they are, the witch and the evil spirit that follows her around." The children jeered and ran at Grandmother Anina. Povi stopped and turned around pushing the little boy who was jeering the loudest. "Go away or the evil spirits will come and eat you up!" Povi yelled at them.

Time passed and Grandmother Anina once again became stiff and filled with pain in the cold winter. Povi went into the Pueblo alone. Young men tried to talk to her, but she ignored them. One young man tried to help her with her packages, then he tried to walk with her, but Povi was cold to him so he left her alone. When she arrived home she told of this experience to her grandmother.

Grandmother Anina laughed, "You should marry, you should have children. Why don't you let the young man at least talk with you about his life and wishes."

Povi put her hands into the deep folds of her skirt. "My life has been happy, but I could not wish it on another. I would like to have children, but I could never live with a man." Povi went outside.

The cold winds blew hard. The people of the Pueblo decided to gather all the pinons they could to help them through the winter. Povi and Grandmother Anina were not invited to go on the pinon harvest. Povi picked up her basket calling out to her grandmother. "I am going to gather pinon. I will be back before the sun rises again."

Grandmother had already told Povi that she did not like this idea for the people from the Pueblo could sneak up and hurt Povi leaving her to die alone in the forest. Povi though, was strong willed and so she went carrying her basket. Povi walked all day and kept to the east of the Pueblo people. She stopped to pick pinon when she saw a good quantity of nuts. She soon wearied.

The basket was heavy and the picking of the nuts was frustrating. Most of the ones on the ground were already eaten by worms or birds. The pinon in the trees were covered with pitch. The pitch also stuck to her hands. The sap was on all her fingers. At last she sat down under a tall pinon tree. It was laden with nuts, but the closest nut was on a branch that was too high for her to reach. Povi sat down under the tall pinon tree, her back sore from bending and reaching. She could hear the sing-song voices from the Pueblo people as they picked their pinon nuts. Povi rubbed her hands together trying to get the sticky sap off them. They burned as she pressed them together. The sap would have to come off if she was to pick more pinon.

A streak of sunlight came down between the trees and touched her hands. The pitch magically melted off.

"DO NOT FOLLOW THE PUEBLO PEOPLE.
THE PATH FOR YOUR PEOPLE IS WITHIN
YOUR SPIRIT.
GO HOME AND PURIFY ALL THAT
YOU TOUCH, PURIFY THAT WHICH
IS WITHIN YOU!!"

Povi stood up, the voice was so loud it sounded like someone up in the tree yelling down at her with a booming voice.

"BE STILL, FEEL THE BREATH OF
MOTHER EARTH. PREPARE A CIRCLE OF
ROUNDNESS — FROM YOU
LIFE WILL GROW."

Povi gathered up her baskets of pinon nuts. The sun's rays followed her home wrapping themselves around her as she walked. Grandmother Anina sat at the table. Povi explained to her grandmother what had happened in the forest. Grandmother Anina moved all of their belongings out of the home, building a lean-to near the horno. Grandmother Anina kept the fire burning in the horno all day and into the night.

Povi washed in the water her grandmother heated. Then she spent four days washing, scrubbing and cleaning their home. After the four days Povi crawled to her Grandmother Anina and fell into a deep sleep. Two days went by with Povi sleeping. Grandmother Anina watched the mud home. No one came, no one disturbed them.

On the evening of the third day Povi awoke. She ate the stew her grandmother had prepared for her. "Grandmother Anina, let us see what the purifying has brought us."

The grandmother was hesitant. "Povi, you should wait for a vision before you enter."

Povi smiled, "I have had a vision."

Povi walked into the mud home. She pushed back the blanket in the door opening. White corn fell at her feet. She picked it up and examined the fat juicy ears of corn. The kernels glowed in the twilight.

Grandmother took the corn from Povi, "How can we live in a home full of corn?"

Povi laughed, "I will move it to the shed."

She walked around the home to the other door. She pulled back the blanket that hung in the doorway. Large brown pinon nuts rolled to the ground. Povi lifted up a handful and gave them to Grandmother Anina. A very large pinon nut rolled down from the tall pile to Povi's eye level. She picked it up and without taking off the shell, popped it into her mouth and swallowed it. Her body warmed with the taste, her face glowed with the good feeling it generated inside her body.

Povi and Grandmother Anina never had want of corn or pinon nuts again. Povi took the white corn to the Pueblo and traded it for other goods they needed. The children danced around Povi calling her, "Gue-cha-ayuh," or Queen of the White Corn.

In the fall when the leaves started to turn gold, Povi gave birth to a baby boy. Sun rose early that morning and watched his child enter the world. Sun shone down his rays of approval. The people in the village had been ready for the baby of the evil woman. The Cacique had already been notified. He arrived in the plaza to announce the birth of the baby for he had sent out spies to watch Povi and Grandmother Anina. The people danced and chanted all night coming closer and closer to Povi's home. Povi prayed with all her might that her son might be spared. On the fourth day the Cacique arrived. "It is by order of this Pueblo that you tell us who the father of this boy is?"

Povi spoke clearly, "Sun Spirit is the father of this baby, you cannot take him away."

The Cacique challenged her. "It could not be the sun's baby, for he would have told the Elders. This child must be put to death."

The Cacique took the baby out of Povi's arms. The other people held her by the shoulders so that she could not follow. The Cacique carried the baby to the sacred arroyo and threw him into the rocky sand calling out, "The spirits that brought this one into this life will let him live or they will let him die." The Cacique threw blue cornmeal over the screaming baby, then he and the other people left. Sun watched with his golden eyes. Sun called the deer from the forest and sent them to get his baby. The strongest stag deer in the forest led his does to the baby. The stag lowered his head and with his antlers newly covered with winter velvet, gently lifted the baby up and carried him in his horns. The does stood around the stag making soft grumbling sounds. The baby stopped crying. The does made a crib for the baby out of grass and they nursed him with their milk. The baby grew.

In the early evening the stag would leave the forest and go to the arroyo. He would stand there with his head up high and listen. His ears would perk up at the song:

"My son, far from his Pueblo is,

He cries there and I cry here,

Ay-n,n, Cillana, my dear son.

Ay-an, A-yan, Pa'ay."

Povi would sing this song just before the sun would go down. The stag would run back into the forest and nudge the baby boy, making a deep resonating sound in his throat and the baby would chortle. The boy grew older, bigger, and wise in the ways of the forest. The stag never left the boy's side.

One day, a Pueblo boy was walking through the forest. He stopped to rest under a tree. He heard some singing. He looked for the person singing and barely got a glance of a wild boy running naked through the forest with a herd of deer. The singing was more beautiul than the Pueblo boy had ever heard before. He ran back to the Pueblo and told the Elders of what he had heard and seen. The Cacique gathered several men from the Pueblo who were good trackers and set off into the forest. They tried to catch the wild boy.

The first day, they heard him sing; the second day, they found tracks; the third day they saw him running and on the fourth day they captured him. The boy had the same features as Povi, his beauty was astounding. The boy could not speak in words that they could understand. This made the Pueblo men angry and they shoved the boy to the ground. The boy let out a loud wail. Sun formed a beam of light around the boy.

"THIS IS MY SON,

HE BELONGS TO YOUR PUEBLO.

HE WILL BE YOUR KING.

HE IS NOT TO SEE A WOMAN, LIGHT,

NOR FIRE FOR FOUR DAYS.

IF YOU DISOBEY HE SHALL BE RETURNED TO ME.

YOU SHALL TREAT HIM WELL FOR HE IS YOUR KING."

The men knelt down in front of the boy. The boy's eyes opened wide and he opened his mouth to speak. He could then be understood. The Cacique sent his runners to the Pueblo telling them to fix the mud hut in the center of the Pueblo so that it would be without sunlight, also to post a guard and put all the women in the kiva until the boy was safe on the fourth day.

Three days went by and the boy had been kept in the room without any light, fire, or women. The wife of one of the Elders decided that she wanted to be the first to see the wild boy. She got up in the middle of the night while it was still dark. The guard at the kiva did not see her leave. She was shaking with anticipation, now at last she could hold a rank among the women of the Pueblo for she would be the first woman to see the wild boy.

She felt along the side of the mud hut. She knelt down on the ground. The guard was her uncle, he would be angry with her if he found her here. She held her breath, she found the window opening. There it was, the thick blanket. She slowly inched behind the blanket into the window. She pulled the flint from her belt along with a long wax candle. She sparked the flint, lit the candle and crept into the room.

The boy was sound asleep. The woman moved ever so quietly around the bedroll to see the boy's face. He was beautiful. The boy opened his eyes. He opened his mouth to speak, then it all happened so fast . . .

He was no longer a boy, but a young buck deer. The room was closed then, the wall behind the woman fell away. The boy jumped from the bed a young buck deer and he ran through the night. The woman was not sure which had happened first. She stood there with all the fear of the world in her being. The boy, the young buck deer and the wall were gone. There standing before her was her uncle. He was yelling and shouting. There were people everywhere. What had she done? She dropped to the floor.

The young buck deer ran out into the forest. He cried out and his hooves thundered across the land. The stag awoke from his sleep, he rose up on his long legs and let out a rolling cry. The young buck deer ran through the forest, now sure of his path home. He ran to the stag. The stag put his head on the young buck's neck. The deer were now reunited.

Povi awoke in the night hearing the deer call out to each other. She ran to the door in time to see a splendid young buck deer leap the arroyo and gallop for the forest. She knew it was over. Her son was now gone from her forever. Povi knelt in the sand. She put her head down, she was no more.

In the morning, Grandmother Anina searched for Povi but all she found was a single ear of majestic white corn lying on the edge of the arroyo. Around the ear of corn were Povi's clothes. Her moccasins were imprinted with the symbol of the sun. Povi was now at peace, alone forever.

Ya ha hine ko' O' O' O' . . .

Grandfather's voice broke the stillness. He was not one to be forgotten. "Nee-nee, are you in there? Are you in the ice-box house?" He pushed his way into the widow's home. "Here you are." He sat down next to me on the couch. "Tea? You are drinking tea?" He touched the tea pot. "Cold tea?" His eyes sparkled at the widow.

The widow smiled. "It was once hot. Would you like some hot tea?"

Grandfather laughed. "All right, but I don't have all day." He pulled on my braid. "I thought you wandered off to the Testing Ground." Grandfather pulled out a long smelly cigar. He went through all of his pockets. "I know I have some matches in here somewhere."

The widow came back into the room. "Here, you left these here last time you came for tea."

Grandfather cleared his throat. "You kept them that long?"

The widow smiled. "Two days isn't long." Grandfather lit his cigar.

"Where's the Testing Ground?" I asked.

The widow frowned. "It is not a good place to be alone."

Grandfather cleared his throat. "Nonsense. Nee-nee can handle the Testing Ground. If I took her into the forest for a week, she could take on the worst test there is." The kettle in the kitchen started to whistle. The widow left the room.

"You have never heard the story of the Testing Ground? Would you like me to tell it to you?"

The widow brought in a tray with cookies, cream and sugar. Grandfather smiled, showing all his teeth. He took four cookies putting them into his mouth all at once.

"Now I shall tell you of the Testing Ground. Here, take some tea, try these cookies. Here, sit back." Grandfather loaded up a white napkin with all he thought I needed. He winked at the widow. His cigar glowed as he spoke.

3

STONES OF WISDOM

The old grey haired mother knelt near her daughter. The sun was slowly coming up on the horizon. The fire had died down and the boy in the corner of the summer hut was breathing quietly. He was not asleep, but his eyes were tired. He watched his mother. Her eyes were shut, her breathing soft, almost not there at times. The bloody gash on her forehead was wrapped with a wet cloth. His mother spoke once during the night, not to him, but to his grandmother. He had not heard the words, but the smile on her face was enough for him to know she was moving on to another land.

His grey haired grandmother sighed. She nodded her head towards him and pointed to the fire. He silently crept out into the dawn. He walk-ed to the forest and gathered sticks. The air was fresh, the forest busy with life. He remembered his mother and hurried back to the mud hut. His grandmother reached for his arm and pulled him to her. He knelt, watching his mother's face. Her lips were closed, her eyes peaceful. Grandmother removed the bandage from the wound and threw it into the fire. She then leaned back on her feet, rocking on her knees as she began to chant.

The boy shook his head. Tears welled up in his eyes, he ran through the forest to the rock cliff. Eagles soared, swallows called out, the sun met his cry. Sun shone down its warmth on the boy. The warmth brought with it the reminder that he was still needed to help his mother into the next world. He found a long stick from the forest and started digging. He dug a deep hole near the forest path. He dug all day.

Grandmother filled small pots with cornmeal and fresh bread. She washed the moccasins her daughter wore. By sundown the hole was ready and all the needed items were collected. The two of them carried the woman to the hole. They placed pinon under her, put the pots of cornmeal and fresh bread around her head and placed the moccasins near her feet. They covered her with pinon, sage and some juniper. The boy and his grandmother chanted into the night.

Before the sun rose, when the sky was pink orange with light, the boy and his grandmother covered the woman's body with dirt and corn-meal dust from the fire.

"Grandmother, would you tell me of my father?"

"Not, it is not my place to tell you of him."

"Who can tell me of my father's ways?"

"No one who knows you. You are to know of your mother's purpose in life." The grandmother stood up. "It is time for us to move on." She gathered up their belongings. Adan helped her with the bedrolls.

"Grandmother, my years are many, almost fifteen and I have no knowledge of my father. There must be something . . ."

"Hush, we must move on to another place. Carry these and be careful of your thoughts." They walked on in silence. Grandmother sat down to rest under a tall cottonwood tree.

"Your mother was raised in the north, in the Pueblo of the Horses. Your mother was a beauty and admired by all who knew her. My husband, your grandfather, worked hard for the horse men. He never touched the horses of the Spanish, only the horses that were used in the fields. This was quite an honor. Your mother learned to ride on these horses in the field. She would sing of horses and she lived for the day when she could have a horse of her own."

Grandmother tossed her bundles over a stream, carefully following on fallen branches. "Your father was once a great warrior, he was a man of great wealth. You have his eyes and his walk."

Adan interrupted her, "Was my father killed fighting the Spanish?"

"No, he was not one of the many who were killed. Your grandfather fought them to his death." They walked on in silence. The sun began to go down over the tall hills. A stream gurgled near them. Grandmother dropped her bundles and knelt for a drink. Adan carefully looked around for other people.

Grandmother sat back on her heels. "Your father named you with a Spanish name so that if you were taken prisoner you might have a chance to escape. Your mother's sister, my youngest daughter, was taken to the big home of the Spanish men. She was made a woman to more than one man. Her name was Tinini, she was a beauty like your mother. The Spanish took many girls away from their homes. We never saw them again although we did hear that they had children by the Spanish men."

They walked along a mountain trail. Quail and rabbits bounded out of their way. The tall cottonwood trees nodded in gentle breezes that followed them. A large raven dove down in front of them, watching them move past him. Grandmother tired quickly. Her white hair was now falling down her back, she pulled a long wooden stick from her thick hair and rewound it. "There is more to carry without your mother's help. Your mother worked hard for us, she fell a long way off that cliff."

Adan nodded, he had been looking for berries when he heard his mother cry out. She had busied herself picking pinon, lost her footing and fallen down a steep cliff. The thick brush near the edge had blocked her view where she was destined to fall. His mother had been very tired from the long walk through the night, then they had spent the morning making the mud hut where she had died.

Adan's life had always been one of a nomad. He could not ever remember a place where they had stayed for longer than two nights. The coldest winters were endured by moving from one shelter to another. His mother had made lean-to's, mud huts, even wooden structures for them. His mother provided a lot of the food, and kept them all well with her herbs and teas.

Adan picked some berries offering them to his grandmother. "Why must we move all the time? Why can't we stay in the Pueblo like those people we met last full moon?"

Grandmother shook her head, "Adan, you ask too many questions."

Grandmother pulled her bundles to her chest and moved up to higher ground. The path she chose was in the darkest part of the forest. He had not seen such a dismal place. The forest was overgrown with dark vines. The branches on the junipers hung down low to the path so they had to crawl in places to get through the brush. Birds flitted overhead screaming at them. Snakes slithered in the thick wet grass. Crickets chirped after they passed. A thick cloud of flying bugs attacked them at the clearing. Adan stared out in wonder. A black raven sat on a large stone watching. Grandmother crawled under some chamisa bushes dropping her bundles on the other side. Adan followed. Certainly his grandmother would not want to spend the night here.

She did. She rolled out the bedrolls, unwrapped the flour bags, scooped up dry pinon needles for a fire. Adan knew what he had to do; he lay the other bundles near her, wiped off his hands and started searching for firewood. He had to crawl out of the clearing where his grandmother was busy preparing food.

On the other side of them was a beautiful clear crystal pond with a spring at the top. Adan washed. The pond was so clear that he could see beautiful round shiny stones on the bottom. He reached down and pulled out a handful to examine. They were hard black stones. They would make good points for his spear. He could sharpen them later. A long black feather fell into the pond rippling Adan's reflection. He hurried back.

Grandmother had a large fire going when he returned. She had burned some of the flour bags and had hot cakes and hot atole ready for dinner. Grandmother's eyes sparkled in the firelight. "Do you know where we are?" she asked him.

"No, I don't remember this place." Adan lay back on his bedroll full and content.

"This is the place of finding. You will honor your mother here and in return you will find your honor. This will be your Testing Ground." Grandmother let her hair loose unrolling it to the ground. She rubbed it with her fingers.

"Too many evil spirits have threatened our lives. It is up to you to save our people from any more harm." She scooped up a bowl of corn-meal rubbing it over her tired, wrinkled body. Adan turned away leaving her to her privacy of thought and tradition. He lay back on his bedroll searching the sky for the stars of Father Sky. Brother Moon shone through the thick trees peering down at him.

Grandmother started to sing: "Oh, Great Spirits, with songs in my heart I say now that this tree was slow to bloom — This young man you see here and I have fallen away — Here I stand old and withered — Here his is young and unused. I recall the vision you sent — Nourish this young leaf so that it may bloom and fill with birds — He can go to the Sacred Circle to find the proud road to his People."

Brother Moon listened to the thoughts of the grandmother. He watch-ed the feelings of Adan in the smoke. Moon shook his yellow head and a large object fell to Mother Earth. Father Sky shook his blanket with the holes in it and spirits from long ago fell through landing near the object of the Moon. The object was still when it landed on Mother Earth. Then slowly it began breathing. Holes in the side of the object began forming. Eyes appeared. Small triangles lifted up on its head to form ears. These ears grew, they became larger than the object. From the side of the object a hole formed. It opened wider and wider. The large hole opened completely to reveal sharp pointed objects. A drool of spittle flowed from this tremendous mouth. Two smaller holes formed above the mouth of teeth to let out a smelly foaming fire. This dripped on the ground around the large floppy ears.

The Sky Spirits of long ago raced around this object of horror. They ran far enough away to tease it. The object pushed itself to them using its long ears. In one swift movement it captured these spirits and gobbled them up. The spirits took on a human shape and ran to the camp of Adan and his grandmother. "Help us, help us, there is a spirit out there that has attacked our people and is eating them up."

Grandmother raised her eyes to the sky. Moon glowed down around her. Adan felt the courage within him rise. He picked up his spear. He took two stones that he had sharpened before dinner and placed them on his stick, wrapped them quickly with rawhide and double tied it with his teeth. Stealthily he moved away from the fire.

Then he saw the evil spirit eating a human spirit, the foamy, fiery spittle dripping on the ground leaving a path wherever the creature went. The eyes glowed with hunger and moved towards Adan. He lifted his spear ready for the attack. The evil spirit opened its tremendous mouth crushing the spear. Adan stood with a broken stick in his hand. Adan grabbed one of the human spirits and pulled it into the forest with him. "Where did this spirit come from? Did he follow you here?"

The human spirit cringed at Adan's harsh words. The human spirit ran from him calling out, "You are afraid of it. You are afraid with no pride." Adan shook his head, he was afraid, but he still had his pride. The evil spirit was indeed an awful sight and smelled worse. Death was not what Adan wanted to face on this night of trial.

Adan moved back to the fire to find his grandmother watching him. She was kneeling, crying, "You are like your father. You would feed me to the evil spirits rather than face danger yourself."

Adan turned away from her. He would use his wisdom; to rush into fight something one did not understand was not wise. Adan would use his knowledge of life to guide him in killing the creature. Adan sat down on his bedroll. He pulled out the stones he had found from the crystal clear pond. He knocked them together sharpening them. The clicking sound echoed through the forest's night air.

"You will bring that creature here and he will eat us up, you must be quiet. If you have no honor at least let us live until daylight," Grandmother whispered harshly to him.

Adan continued to knock the stones together. He sharpened them knife sharp. They were small stones, not large enough to use for a spear on the large creature.

Grandmother whispered again, "Please stop that sound. The creature draws nearer to us all the time. You are drawing him into the forest. Adan, stop that."

Adan continued. Father Sky peered through one of his star holes in the night blanket of the sky. Brother Moon smiled to himself. The boy was thinking silently. Silence of thought brought the best thoughts to the surface. Suddenly, Grandmother gasped pointing to the chamisa bush near the clearing. Adan turned to watch her. Fear filled her face.

"Grandmother, you must be strong for both of us. Believe in me and it will give me strength. If you turn on me you will drain me of my wisdom. You must believe that my mother taught me well." Adan stood tucking the sharp stones into his belt. The creature breathed hard on the chamisa bush burning it with his foaming nose. Adan rushed at it screaming.

The creature backed out of the forest. Grandmother closed her eyes. Adan stepped out into the clearing to face the creature; instead he was met with an open mouth of teeth.

Adan was swallowed up, disappearing into the tremendous mouth of the creature. The human spirits hurried to the grandmother. They turned into a light blue smoke and wrapped themselves around her. As they did so they told her that her grandson was swallowed by the creature. Grandmother listened to them but in her heart she turned her doubts to strength. "I believe that Adan will survive. He is strong, he will win. Adan is not gone . . . he is wise, he will win." The spirits laid her down on the bedroll and let her sleep a deep slumber until morning.

Birds flitted around the dying fire. Their screeching woke up grandmother. She rolled up her bundles crying, "Adan, you betrayed me. Now, I will be eaten by the creature with no one here to protect me. Our traditions will be gone."

"Grandmother, you speak too soon. Your faith in me is not very strong, is it?" Adan walked into the clearing. His brown eyes were wide, glowing with strength. His long flowing black hair was filled with golden feathers. He appeared taller, stronger, and he glowed with confidence. "Grandmother, come with me." She followed him. She had become entranced by his magical strength. Out of the forest and on the flatlands lay the creature on its ear, with its guts pouring out onto the ground.

"I let the creature swallow me, then I hurried into its throat carefully missing the sharp pointed teeth. I cut up its insides with my sharp stones. It took all night. The human spirits that were inside are all free."

Grandmother let Adan carry all the bundles for he did so without difficulty. He lifted her over the streams and through the heavy brush. They walked for four days until they came to a Pueblo.

The Pueblo was having a dance ceremony when they entered. The Elders stopped chanting when they saw Adan and his grandmother enter the plaza. Pride swelled in grandmother's bosom as the people turned to watch Adan. His beauty and strength mixed with his youth were awesome.

The Elder at the front of the chanting line came up to greet them. "P'in P'oe, welcome back to your Pueblo. We have longed for your family to return to us."

Grandmother smiled back at the Elder, "This is my grandson, Adan. His name is Spanish, but now he has become one of us. He killed an evil creature that was sent down to test him. His name shall now be 'Tsee', for he has the knowledge of the great black stone."

They were welcomed into the Pueblo and a great feast was given in their honor. Adan Tsee learned of his father's disloyalty to the Indian people in order to gain wealth from the Spanish soldiers. The Spanish had fled the Pueblo when an uprising occurred years ago. The people were now in search of a wise one to guide their Pueblo back to good health. Adan Tsee taught many the way of his wisdom and showed them the healing that his mother had taught him. His grandmother found her home still solid for her to have a long life.

Adan married a young woman, Nan-Povi. She was the daughter of an Elder who had died in the fight for the Pueblo's freedom. They named their daughter after Tinini who was lost to the Spanish. Adan had many tests and trials that he had to pass before being totally accepted by his people. He never lost his courage or his strength.

Brother Moon still watches down over him.

Grandfather smiled at me. "That is the Testing Ground. Do you think that you would be wise enough to pass the test?" His eagerness to make me say something I did not wish to was interrupted by the honking of a truck horn. Grandfather stood up peering out of the window.

"Leroy is here. He wants to take the dogs to the vet. I'll be back. Keep the tea warm." Grandfather set his cigar down on the edge of the wooden table. He disppeared out the door. We could hear him yelling to Leroy as he ran to his home.

"Your grandfather remembers the stories well. He changes them a little each time he tells them, which keeps them from getting boring. One time we had a government man come out to count all the Indians in this area. Your grandfather took him aside and told him that many of the people who live here were not people at all. He explained to the government man that spirits take on many forms and they can easily be confused for people. Sometimes the children or even adults will appear to talk to imaginary ghosts when they are actually talking to the spirits that guide them."

The widow and I built a fire in the corner fireplace. "Do you know the story of the children that disappeared and came back with the knowedge of another world?"

"I know of a story that most women and mothers should know. The story of The Journey."

"Please tell it to me. Grandfather will be busy for some time gathering up all of his dogs."

4

PASSAGE TO WISDOM

Tall cottonwood trees swayed in the wind. Birds chirped in search of a midday meal. A woman sat quietly working. Her daughter played with grass stalks. Stacked willows rested against the woman's knee. One by one they were being used up, carefully held in calloused hands scarred from the sharp willow edges; fingers wove the willows tightly together. The day moved slowly from chirping birds to a young daughter's song of hunger while the mother woman weaving willows in and out over and under did not hear the words of the song.

Long black hair combed, wrapped, pulled up and back framed the mother woman's face. Her dark black eyes peered out of thick black eyelashes. Dark purple cotton graced the mother woman's torso followed with a dark tan skirt. The mother woman's toes were curled into the dirt as she sat on her knees weaving. The movement and action of this mother woman was as natural as the clouds floating across the sky. Peace and tranquility dominated the mood.

Squared off bangs hung over the expression of the sad little girl. Hunger had seized her and she could no longer play or sing. The little girl watched her mother. Her mother was with child. Soon, is what her father had told her, soon she would have someone to play with, maybe someone to eat with, too. The little girl hung over a low juniper branch. The four-year-old entwined her fingers. Her long skinny legs were dirty and scratched, her long skirt torn.

"Mother, it is late. Could we eat?"

"No, not yet. Let's wait a little longer."

"Mother, we have not yet eaten today. The sun is going down. Can I get something from the storage room to eat?"

"No, you can wait. If you do not like to wait you can go and beg for food in the Pueblo." The mother's voice was sharp and hurtful. The little girl was used to this. She walked to the forest and in the dim evening light she looked for pinon nuts. She found enough to keep her busy until the sun was down and the sky was dark. Father Sky covered Mother Earth with his black blanket. This night he peeked down anxious to see this little girl eat a good meal. The little girl quietly walked back to her mother. She was still weaving. The little girl sat down and studied her mother's face.

"What are you doing now? What do you want?" the woman barked at her daughter. The little girl did not answer. "You want some food? All right! I will give you some food and then you can leave me in peace." The mother put her basket aside. It was almost finished. She had started to wrap the edge for the final weaving. Mother stood stretching her legs. "Come I will feed you, P'o-aa."

They walked into the two-room house. The storage room was a small niche behind a hanging blanket. The mother pulled out some corn-meal. She stirred in some water and made a watery mix. Then she took some twigs by the door and headed for the horno. There she built up a fire placing a hot flat rock on top of the horno's side lift. She poured the corn mix into it making a cornmeal pancake. She made ten of them, stacked them, then carried them into the house on a flat basket.

They sat down to eat on the clean mud floor. "Hello, I see that I am just in time for the evening meal." The little girl's father walked into the room.

Mother gasped, "You are so late, I thought you may have eaten in the Pueblo with your friends."

Father lifted up the empty flat basket. "I am not late, where is the meat? I brought home plenty of meat last hunt, where is it?" Father sat down next to his little girl. He patted her head and tickled her.

Mother answered, "Meat? We ate all the meat. There is none left. Besides it takes too long to cook."

"Well, can I have some pancakes?" Father smiled at his woman. Mother sighed. She got up, mixed her cornmeal and went outside to cook pancakes.

"Did your mother feed you today? Did you have a morning meal?" P'o-aa shook her head. That way if her mother accused her of telling, she didn't say a word. "What did Mother do all day? Did she weave?" P'o-aa nodded.

The pancakes were all they had for the evening meal. Father stood up and pulled back the storage blanket. "There is meat here. If I cook it up tonight you can eat it tomorrow and save some for the evening meal. All right?"

Mother had already gone back outside. She was gathering up her willows. Her mood was solemn for she never liked to stop weaving until she was finished. Father and P'o-aa cooked the meat. Some they cut very thin, washed in river water and laid out on a blanket. Long thin strips of meat were covered with juniper berries to keep the birds away until it was dried into jerky. Father sang songs to his daughter and told her of his adventures on the hunting trips. He also told her of the meeting they had with the Elders and the decision to keep trading with the outsiders that were moving closer to their land. Father did not like this idea, but he was only one vote. Father carried his sleepy little girl to her bedroll. She had eaten four helpings of cooked meat. Father pulled the bedroll over her to keep out the cold night air. Father Sky closed his eyes and he too, slept. Mother continued her weaving. She had wrapped the top of the basket with feathers.

Father sat down near her, "You are not teaching our daughter. You only weave from early sun to night." The mother did not answer. Father continued, "In our Pueblo the mother woman teaches her daughter and sons the traditions of her people."

"When I have a son, I can teach them both." Mother cut a long feather into two parts.

Father held mother's wrist. "When are you going to stop weaving and become the mother of your daughter?"

Mother froze, she stared at him. "What do you want? You show me that you want to be an Elder's son and sit in the Pueblo with the other Elders being wise. I weave baskets to trade. Do you want me to stop weaving and raise your children? Then who will support us?" Mother spit the words at him.

"I married you to have you as my woman and the mother of my children. That is the first, most important reason for us to be here. You said you wanted to weave. You told me at one point that you respected my wisdom and that I should use it to help out the Pueblo. I hunt, I trade meat and hides for us, I even cook the meat. Tonight I cooked meat so that our daughter will not go hungry." Father pushed the willows away.

Mother threw the basket against the side of the house. "You are telling me that you do not want me to weave? You want me to nurse the four-year-old girl and the new baby. I am not here only for them. I must do what makes me feel good. I was taught to weave and the Great Spirits want me to weave or they would stop me." She frowned.

"How do you want the spirits to stop you? Do you need a sign from them? Look at your little girl, P'o-aa. She is our child, not a wandering animal. She is always hungry. Hungry for a mother, for other children to play with, for food and care."

36

"Fine then, you give it to her. I am busy doing what I must do in my life." Mother stood up. Her back hurt. Her large belly made her tired.

Father stood up next to her, rubbing her back. "You are a mother woman now, times have changed. You are no longer alone to decide for yourself. You must share your time, your work, your cooking, and your life with your family. The choice was yours and you took it."

Mother bent down and carefully lifted the basket. "Here, it is finished. You can get the baby a new blanket and a doll for this. It only took me one day. The others would take a long time to make any basket of this quality." Mother handed it to father, then went into the home. Father stroked the basket, thinking.

The days moved on, one after another. Some days there was food and fun with father. Other days father would stay in the Pueblo for he was wise and the Elders wanted his opinion. Mother wove her baskets. They were traded for good things. The Pueblo Elders appreciated her hard work for it brought prestige to their Pueblo. Father liked the prestige of a great weaver in the family.

One night when the moon was only partly there, mother started crying out in pain. Father was not there. P'o-aa got up and ran to her mother. She was cautious for she knew her mother could get angry easily. Mother called out to her, "Go to the Pueblo and get your grandmother. Go now quickly, ask her to bring the Pu'fona."

P'o-aa ran as fast as she could. She found her grandmother's home only by chance for it was very dark that night. Grandmother told her to stay with grandfather. Grandfather carried P'o-aa to the kiva and told her father that the baby his woman carried was coming.

P'o-aa stayed many days with her grandparents. Grandfather showed P'o-aa how to make atole on a kitchen fire. They ate it all up scooping it into bread. Grandfather had fresh goat's milk which he heated for her. "I remember when your mother was little, she loved to eat fresh bread and drink warm milk before bed. Then I would carry her into her room, like this, and put her down on her warm blanket and tell her a story of the old days."

Grandfather leaned back on one arm and told the little girl about his life as a boy. She soon fell sound asleep.

P'o-aa learned a lot from her grandfather. Grandfather also learned that his daughter was not teaching P'o-aa the ways of the people. Grandmother came home and asked P'o-aa to stay with them until after the mother's cleansing ceremony, Kuliohatsiper, Kudioaniyima, and the Kuriohatsipe.

The time for her to go back to her own home came sooner than she wished. Grandmother took her bedroll and clothing under her arm, pulling P'o-aa as they walked back to the home at the edge of the Pueblo. Mother put down the basket she was weaving when she saw grandmother. She ran to them, talking to grandmother only. The baby lay on the ground wrapped in a warm blanket. The little girl cautiously studied him. He was very small, he was sound asleep. She was grateful for his little body.

Grandmother left shortly after the midday meal. The little girl cleaned up the wooden bowls the way her grandmother had showed her. Mother lay down on her bedroll with the baby. P'o-aa started sweeping out the front room. Sun moved across the sky letting the cool fall wind blow the leaves around. Mother got up, handing the baby to the little girl. Mother went out back to examine her willows that were soaking. P'o-aa carried her brother around the home.

The scream from the baby's mouth that penetrated the air was frightening. The baby screamed loud and long. P'o-aa hurried out of the home with the baby boy carefully in her arms. "Mother, Mother, the baby, the baby!" Mother was not there. P'o-aa felt tears roll down her cheeks. "Mother, Mother, where are you?" There was no reply. P'o-aa sat down with her back against the warm mud wall of their home. She rocked the baby boy, she cooed to him, she bounced him, but he didn't stop crying.

"Mother, Mother, what do I do with the baby? Mother, your baby is hungry, Mother, Mother where are you?" P'o-aa cried holding the unhappy little baby in her arms. The four-year-old leaned her head back searching the sky. "Father said the spirits are always with us, little one. Spirits, help the baby, help." P'o-aa hugged her little brother as she spoke.

Sun shone down sending a ray of light to the baby's mouth, Father Sky filled the ray of sunlight with sweet pollen. The baby stopped crying. He munched the sweet thick pollen in his toothless mouth. Then he opened his mouth for more. Sun warmed the baby and he soon fell asleep. The little girl watched with great amazement. She knew this was great magic.

Mother returned, coming up the path from the spring as father met P'o-aa on his way home from the Pueblo. The dried tears on his daughter's face told him what he needed to know. Mother stopped short of bumping into him.

"I had to go to the spring for more willow. I did not mean to be gone all afternoon."

"You were gone all afternoon? Who fed the baby? Who is this

baby's mother?" Father was angry. His face was flushed. He pushed his palms together for he knew that it was not his place to question his woman or her ways.

Mother took the baby from P'o-aa, "I have been careful with him, look he is not even hungry. I knew that our daughter would be good in caring for him. Look how peacefully he sleeps."

Father took his leather pouch off his shoulder, "What is for the evening meal?" Mother hurried outside to get her willow into the water to soak.

P'o-aa came into the home. "I have some dried meat and this morning at grandmother's I baked bread. I will have the meal prepared soon."

The evening meal was eaten in silence. The baby was sleeping, no one had anything to say nor did they want to say anything that might wake the baby.

The days moved on. P'o-aa worked hard and her mother seemed to be in a better mood. She didn't get angry for days, then she would storm and yell, but the anger did not bother the little girl any more. She would pick up her baby brother and rock him. They would go into the forest and she would tell him of the Great Spirits. The baby would smile, then P'o-aa would sing to him of the ways of magic. P'o-aa cooked the meals while the baby slept. The baby did not grow very fast so the four-year-old could easily carry him on her back while looking for wood.

On one particular morning, P'o-aa came back from the forest to find several Elders sitting around mother. The little girl knew that she would not be invited to listen, so she took the baby into the home. She sang and cooked the meal. The Elders left before the sun started to set. The little girl took her brother to mother to nurse. Mother grabbed the baby from the girl without speaking. This was not a good sign.

Father came home singing with many stories to tell. The hunters had agreed to go on a hunt the following morning for the air was cold. Winter was on its way. Mother did not speak. Father gathered up his knife and spears. He rubbed animal fat into his moccasins. Mother washed his hair, then wrapped it tightly with pine. P'o-aa fell asleep with her little brother.

P'o-aa was awakened by the sound of men's voices. The other hunters had arrived. Father came in and gave P'o-aa some sacred corn-meal in a cotton bag. "Keep this, if you need anything go to the river. The river will help you. My father gave this to me when I was small but I never used it. I shall be gone for many days, perhaps you will need this." Father patted her head.

"Father, you will be gone long. If I do need help should I go to grandmother's?"

Father shook his head, "If you need help take this bundle and go to the river. I am not sure what it will do, but it has strong powers. My father knew of the ways of those who lived long ago. P'o-aa, you will be safe. Your mother is very quiet, be careful." Father's eyes were bright with feeling. He said more with his smile than with his words. Then he stood tall over her and with a wave of his hand he was gone.

P'o-aa dressed, then went in to see her mother. Mother was wrapping her hair. She was restless, her hands shook. P'o-aa was fearful.

Mother called to P'o-aa, "I have to go into the Pueblo this day and weave for a certain ceremony. I will be in the kiva." P'o-aa studied her mother's face. She was stern, the wrinkles on her forehead were deep. She continued, "I could not tell your father for he would not have approved of a woman going into the kiva."

"You are going into the kiva?" P'o-aa never heard of a woman being allowed into the kiva unless it was for a very serious reason or a great honor.

"Yes, they want me to weave a basket for a sick Elder in the kiva while the medicine man performs the cleansing ceremony. I must do it. It is very important."

P'o-aa helped her mother with her long hair. It took a lot of wool to wrap it and roll it up into a chongo. "What about baby brother? He will get hungry?"

Mother pulled the wool tightly around the rolled hair. "You will bring the baby to the opening of the kiva and call down to me. I will come up and feed him. Don't bring him too often or it will interrupt the Kwantuka ceremony."

Mother gathered up all her willow withes. She tied them in a bundle. the three of them set off for the Pueblo.

"Mother, we did not bring any food for the day. Should I go back and get some?"

Mother shook her head, "No, it is late. I shall weave quickly, it will not be too long. We can go home and cook when this is over. For now, let us stay on our path."

She patted her daughter and the baby on the head when they reached the kiva. Then she descended into the kiva, her chanting mixed with the p'ingxeng chanter.

P'o-aa felt in her pocket. The bag of cornmeal was still there. Baby brother slept. She played with sticks. The other girls in the Pueblo were busy with their chores. Some would stop and talk to her, but then they had to get back to their work.

Baby brother woke up and started crying. The sun was moving across the sky. It was time for him to nurse. P'o-aa gathered up the baby and his blankets. She called out at the kiva ladder, "Mother, it is time to feed the baby." There was no answer. P'o-aa could hear the men chanting. She waited, the baby started playing with his moccasin string on his foot. Then the baby started sucking on his hand and crying. "Mother, it is time to feed the baby," P'o-aa called down again.

Her mother came up the ladder, her voice filled with anger. "Wait a little longer." Mother disappeared.

P'o-aa bounced the baby on her shoulder. The baby kept crying. Finally P'o-aa took some leather from the baby's moccasin and let him suck on it. P'o-aa nervously looked around her, others in the Pueblo were watching her with the little baby. P'o-aa let the baby scream, he would get tired and go to sleep.

The sun moved across the sky. P'o-aa was hungry now, too. The baby had fallen asleep, but every now and then he would let out a howl. P'o-aa gathered up her little brother.

She stamped hard on the kiva roof. "Mother, your son needs to nurse. Please come up and nurse him."

The reply came from down under her, "Wait a while longer. Wait."

P'o-aa shifted the baby from one hip to the other. His little legs bumped the cotton bag in her pocket. She reached into her skirt pocket. Food was what she needed now. Her baby brother's lips were dry and bleeding. His eyes were red and swollen from crying. P'o-aa's arms burned from carrying him, her shoulders ached from holding up his little body against her four-year-old chest. The bundle father had given her would help them. She would take the bundle of sacred cornmeal to the river. P'o-aa walked down the river road path. The bundle empowered her spirit. It carried her down the river road with great swiftness. Her brother's crying did not bother her. She moved quickly around the people coming back from the river.

"P'o-aa, where are you going?" an old grandmother asked her.

"Into the river, into the river," P'o-aa answered.

The old grandmother ran to the Pueblo. She called down the kiva to mother. "Your daughter is going into the river with your baby."

Mother hurried up the ladder, pulled up her long skirt and ran down the river path road.

P'o-aa came to the river. Brother stopped crying. The water was high, the torrents of waves were hitting hard against the shore. P'o-aa lifted her brother onto her shoulder and with careful steps walked into the river. She smiled at the people around her, baby brother smiled, too. They walked down, down, down, into the cold river water. The bright orange sunset glowed on their brown hair as they disappeared.

Mother came to the river's edge. She saw the two brown heads disappear into the water. The fast river current covered them washing a little moccasin downstream. Mother screamed holding her hands in the air, "P'o-aa, wait, wait, wait, wait, wait, I am here. I am here now. P'o-aa wait. You could have waited a little longer." Mother's words fell on the silence of the river's water flowing. Tears flowed down mother's face. Her children were gone.

"Ai-wi, nawa, awi nawa."

Mother went back to the kiva. She gathered up her basket. The sick Elder was asleep. The ceremony had been completed while she was gone. Mother took her willows to the river. She threw them in, watching them float away down into the roaring current.

Golden rays of sun wrapped around the floating bodies. Golden lights shimmering, sliding in movement gathered around the girl and her baby brother. The lights kept them warm in the cold water. The golden lights turned into slivered gold threads. The girl and her brother were turned over and over and over in the fast moving water. The water gurgled with delight. Mother Earth opened up a wide mouthed cave. The golden threads fell away to make a beautiful rug on the floor of this magnificent cave. The cave was filled with large pots of cornmeal, freshly baked bread, open honeycombs oozing with honey, and fresh milk in dripping skins. The girl lay her brother down under the dripping skins of milk. The milk dripped deliciously into his mouth at each request. P'o-aa reached for bread which was tender and moist. She swallowed it as fast as her hands could grab. Water gushed by outside their cave making a soft whirling sound. Their stomachs filled with food, the thread wrapped around them in warmth, the soft flowing sound of the water rocked them to sleep. The sleep was of warm green places. Moon's face was that of a fat orange pumpkin, the wind laughed at the baby's smile, Father Sky wrapped them tighter with his golden blanket. Mother Earth sighed with their presence inside her.

Time wove on through more time. The baby relaxed, P'o-aa smiled in her sleep. Safety, security, acceptance was silent around them. The spirits were there, they cared, they held them and their lives in importance. Water rushed on, time grew further ahead, Mother Earth whispered to P'o-aa of things that were yet to come, of things that P'o-aa should know of and what she would later find on her own. Mother Earth sighed in the night. "You, my child, are as important as rain upon the plants. Your spirit is pure in goodness, and your life shall be filled with growth. You must go back and teach those who do not know the importance of feeling; also to know what Father Sky is saying with each passing day and to remember always that we are each here to believe in our own important destiny."

Father Sky rocked the baby brother in his golden thread blanket. Father Sky held him to the knowledge that food is growth and to be hungry is to always want knowledge to be better.

Wisdom is something that is achieved through time, not given to someone out of duty. Sun was high above them watching out for their mother and father. Sun knew that the ways of wisdom do not come from a lesson learned too easily. Sun watched, Moon guarded.

Father had come home days later from his hunt. He had a good hunt with a lot of meat. He brought his meat to the back door calling his woman out to him. She had come out thin and dirty, her hair was down and she had ashes on her face. Father asked her what happened. She would not speak. He took her to the Pueblo and found out what had happened to his children.

They were both filled with great sadness. Father went to the river. "Father Sky, do I wait? Should we wait or have they gone from us forever?" Father Sky did not answer. He was not going to answer. Father took the short path home. He packed all of his belongings and put them outside his home.

He approached his woman and asked her, "What are you going to do? Are you going to stay here?"

She shook her head and held her hands up to him. "I will dream that the spirits will help undo what has been done. I did not mean to hurt our children and the way of magic is stronger than I. They are on their own path now. I will dream that they show me the way to become better. I will leave, also."

Father went up north to learn the ways of healing from an old medicine man. Mother went to a spring in the northwest. She built a lean-to and with her clever woven grass traps she had enough food to make it through the winter. Her nights were bitter cold, her thoughts of peace. The nights were without dreams. The fires smoked a lot. She was thoughtful, filling herself with strength. One night when the wind was not blowing and the fire was low, she closed her eyes. She felt death creeping over her body. She lay down and rested. The dream came, the spirits told her the time to go home was in the spring. She awoke feeling her strength return.

Spring came bringing a plentiful new crop of berries, flowers and new life. Father thought about his woman. Mother worried about her home. Perhaps her children did not disappear in the river, perhaps the dream had a message, perhaps her dream was an ouuwah from another time.

Mother gathered up her food stock, kicked down the lean-to and started for home. Father, too, said good-by and he left with many blessings. Mother and father met on the Pueblo road. They did not talk. They did not acknowledge each other. The walk was tiring. At night they sat down under separate trees.

Father watched his woman chew on an old piece of meat. He reached into his pouch and pulled out bread. "Here, would you like some fresh bread?" Mother felt ashamed in his presence. She shook her head no. They walked on through the night. The sky was dark with no moon. The holes in Father Sky's blanket were few. The night was dark with feelings of warmth. Father and mother held each other up along the way. The need to return was very important to both of them. The spirit of unity was deep inside them, it was moving closer to the surface as Sun broke through the night air. Sun sent purples, pinks and yellows with shooting colors of the rainbow for them to follow.

Smoke filled the horizon. The Pueblo was close to them now. The day was bright with no clouds. Father stopped at the hill, smoke rose from their lonely home. Smoke rising from the horno welcomed them. Father ran to the door opening. "Who is there? This is our home, who is there?" Mother caught his hand pulling him back. Her eyes were bright with fear. A baby cried from within the home. Mother fell to her knees.

P'o-aa came to the door carrying her little brother. He was smiling and playing with a corn husk doll. Mother cried out, father lifted the children in his strong arms. He carried them to their mother.

––––––––––––––––

Grandfather picked up his cigar, "It is time for us to get back to the willow. Tomorrow I have to take you home, we'd better get to work."

I helped the widow take the dishes into the kitchen. She turned to me as we were leaving, "You get your jacket on and leave it on, your grandfather keeps his home too cold. Here are some tortillas that I made last night. They are good with honey."

Grandfather grumbled, "I plan to cook her a good meal tonight."

The widow smiled, "Get him to tell you the tale of the magic hunter. He should tell that story before time forgets it. Have fun with your grandfather."

We ran through the blowing snow to grandfather's home. The fire was now hot orange coals. We went to our work without any talk. The fire, rekindled, snapped and crackled as the snow piled up outside.

"The widow told me you knew the story of the magic hunter?"

"Yes, she told you that."

"Well, would you tell it to me?"

"Nee-nee, you listen to stories all the time. It is important to talk about what is going on in the world today, too."

"Yes, I suppose it is. What is happening in the world today?"

"Bad things, too many bad things. People in Beirut held hostage, planes crashing, earthquakes in Mexico . . ."

"Grandfather, there are good things like the Prince and Princess coming to America to talk about peace."

"They spend too much money, it's depressing."

"Tell me something that isn't depressing, Grandfather."

"Fine, I will tell you the story of the magic hunter."

Grandfather leaned back against the thick mud wall of his home, his story began.

5

THE MAGIC HUNTER

There is a forest not far from the plains near La Bajada where the cottonwood trees are so thick that daylight cannot find a way to shine on the bare ground near the river. On one particular evening a young girl ran through this forest without an escort. She ran to meet someone and when she got there, she was alone. The young woman, who was around fifteen years old, called out. There was no reply except that of bushes rustling. The young girl moved to the bushes to see what was moving. She was very brave. She parted the bushes to find white bony fingers reaching up to her. This would have frightened her except that a voice spoke out to her.

"Wait, don't leave yet." The long bony fingers reached out to her. "Please, do wait. The sun is going down, darkness will fill the sky, be patient."

The young girl turned her head away from the voice. Tears welled up in her eyes. "Last night when we met you were so tall and handsome. I had no idea that you had died." Her hands wrapped around each other.

"Wait, do not judge me yet. The sun is now on the horizon. Brother Moon is coming up." The red ball in the sky rolled over into its bed on the horizon. "There, the sun is gone. You may turn now. Look at my face and tell me what you see."

"No, it is a white skull which gives me shudders. I do not want to be a part of death." The young woman pulled her long violet black hair over her shoulder and wrapped it around her wrist. "Please, let me go now. I wish to go home." There was no reply. She cocked her head to listen. There was no sound. Turning quickly to see if he had left, her eyes beheld a handsome strong young man. "You, you are the man that was here last night?"

"Yes, I am. I am the same person." His dark tanned face smiled at

46

her. "I always have the same feelings even though I appear differently during the day."

"What happens during the day? When I came earlier to see you here, you were a skull with small fragile fingers, what has happened to you now?" She stood staring at his handsome face.

"You have gone against your family to come here and that is not right. The next time you come you must come with your parents. I would like to ask them if we could marry. You must come with respect and we can ask them together." The young man turned and disappeared through the trees.

"Wait, do not go. Please, I must ask you . . ." She let the words fall. He had asked her to stay, he wanted to ask for her in marriage. She was in love with a handsome man, but not with a skull. Questions filled her mind as she hurried back to her Pueblo.

Young men greeted her as she quickly walked home. Many wanted to marry her, but her heart was taken. The question was how to tell the others.

"You should not be out late at night alone, Munu. Your father has gone out looking for you. The time has come for you to decide who you will marry." Munu's mother took her into her sleeping room. "You are breaking the customs of our people. This is not good. When the morning comes you must announce to your father who it is you wish to marry."

Munu brushed her long hair with her fingers. "Can the marriage ceremony be at night?"

"What? You want to get married at night? Without the blessing of the sun? Munu, I do not understand why you must be so different from your sisters. You argue and fight with all that we want to give you. You shall have a feast and dance in the middle of the day when the sun is highest. Get some sleep. You can talk with your father in the morning light."

Munu's mother sighed, leaving Munu alone. Munu heard her father come into the room. He was laughing with another man. They were talking about all the suitors Munu had.

"She can be a rich woman if she agrees to marry ThuTs'aa. He can give her the luxuries of the land. P'aa Sen can make beautiful baskets, although he is a strange one. He never talks to the Elders in the Pueblo. Agoyo Ovin is wise with his knowledge of herbs and healing, but he is older than I. Perhaps they would not be blessed with children. Khan Ts'ay is full of life with his stories of great hunting. She should pick him."

Mother spoke, "Hush, you men. Munu came back late again tonight.

She was out walking through the forest. She has a secret with her, something in the forest."

The man that was talking with father spoke in a hushed voice, "There is a story that a skeleton lives in the forest. Once, two young girls went into the forest to pick berries, they talked of men and the passions they felt for them. They found a small boy of great beauty wandering around lost and hungry. The two girls took the boy home and hid him in their bedrolls. That night they fed him and wanted their way with him, but each time they tried to touch him he was so cold that they left him alone. In the morning when they awoke they pulled the bedrolls back and to their surprise all they found was a skeleton. They cried out and ran for help. When they returned the skeleton and the boy were gone. No one has seen him, no one has heard him, they have only heard the story."

Father gave a soft laugh, "Do you believe this?"

The man still spoke quietly, "Yes, for it is believed that he will save the Pueblo from times of trouble. Well, I must go now. I will tell no one of Munu's visits to the forest. We still need to find meat for the winter."

Father walked the man to the door. "We will try another hunting party. There must be some game up in the mountains, three times out and no sign of animals is not good. We might have a hungry winter."

The man left leaving mother and father to talk of the story. Munu closed her eyes. Perhaps the man she loved was this man, perhaps she was to bring him to her Pueblo. She knew that she must be true to the spirits that guide her.

Munu's father woke her telling her to dress quickly, for the men who had asked for her hand in marriage were now gathered outside waiting for her. Munu dressed quietly, taking her time. This did nothing to soothe her father. He was anxious to have his youngest daughter married and in her own home to lead her own life.

Munu hurried to her mother's side. "Mother, is it not right that I should marry the man that the spirits guide me to?"

"Yes, my daughter, now tell your father which of the young men outside has taken your breath away?"

"Mother, none of them are of interest to me. They are all very nice hard working men, but I wish to lead my life with a man who is not here."

Father turned to her, "What? You have allowed us to accept favors from these men and you do not wish any of them for a husband?"

Mother stood up, "Father, you accepted the gifts, not Munu. You may return them. Munu could not marry all of them, the gifts were your idea, not hers." Mother faced Munu. "Tell us then who it is that you have chosen to be your man."

"He is very handsome and strong, during the night. He is very proper and lives in the forest." Munu lowered her voice.

"What do you mean 'during the night'? What of him during the day?" Father's voice boomed.

"I don't know what he does during the day. I do not know his name." Munu felt her face burn.

"You do not know his name, you do not know what he does during the day, and yet you wish to have this man as your husband? Did he ask you to marry him?" Munu nodded yes. "Well, I want to meet this young man right now. He is a man, isn't he?"

"Yes."

Father took Munu into the other room. "I want to meet him now. He should come forward and meet your parents and ask for you to be his woman, he should ask us himself."

Munu remained calm. "We must wait until dark. Then you can ask him." Father shook his head, his eyes red with anger. Mother pulled him away from Munu.

Munu gathered up her work apron and went outside to her sisters. Each one had their chunks of clay near their own earth fire or earth oven. Munu pulled her layered apron up over her head. She would work hard and make beautiful pots to take with her in the evening when they would meet her man.

Munu picked up some animal fat and worked it with her hands. She took her chunk of clay, pouring water on top of it, and began to work. Her sisters whispered around her, Munu pretended she didn't notice.

She took her mano and smashed it into the hard piece of clay. The pieces broke off the clay, she pounded these until they were powder. She took her white cotton cloth and placed it near two or three branches that were used for the purpose of separating out the small stones and rocks from the finer clay. The sun shone down, warming her long arms. "Spirits, help me to be strong," Munu whispered.

"You have not been seen in the Pueblo with the man of your choice, Munu?" Her older sister came over and knelt by her side. "Have you decided who your husband will be?" Munu shook her head indifferently. "Munu, mother is worried about you. She feels you will decide to live with them in their house forever. You are our little sister and we want to help you, but you must let us."

Munu threw her clay up into the air. The heavier pieces fell on the ground, the lighter particles went into her cotton cloth. "I am fine, I will not stay with them forever. There is someone I am very fond of, but I don't think father believes me; he will see tonight."

Munu's sister laughed, "How well I know that feeling. When I wanted to be Ba'a Ta's woman fear crept through me. Father had already given me the names of four men I could choose from and Ba'a Ta's name was not one of them. All night, for many nights, I thought of running away or of giving myself up to father's choosing, then mother came in one night and asked me who I really liked. I told her and she made me tell the true way I felt to father. Munu, you must be true to your own feelings for no one can live your life for you. We care about you and want to see you with many children."

Munu's sisters laughed. They all had become with child in the month of the feast day. All four of her sisters were soon to be rich with family.

Munu gathered up her clay powder and carried it to the matate. There she ground it down once more. Munu mixed her clay powder, adding water to most of the clay as she kneaded the mixture with her hands. Some of the powdered clay she used kept sticking. She rolled out her coils, laid them on her base and shaped a wedding pot. The finished pot was placed with others that she would soon heat in the oven. Munu pulled some soft clay out of the empty water jar. She threw her clay up into the air. The heavier pieces fell on the ground and she started to make another pot. Munu put her pots into the smoldering earth oven, carefully placing them far enough apart so they would not hurt each other if one burst in the heat. Then she covered them over with deer dung. Finished now except for the waiting, Munu set to work to make a special bowl for the handsome man in the forest.

Munu's sisters let out a scream as they pulled pots out of an earth fire. All the pots in one earth oven had broken. The other two earth ovens were still going. Munu hurried over to find out what happened.

"You thought bad thoughts and the fires got too hot. Huu Ts'say, what could you have done to bring this on yourself?" The sisters carefully pulled the broken pots out of the oven.

Munu knelt down filtering carefully through the oven. "Huu Ts'say, you didn't use mica in your clay. Didn't you let your clay dry first?"

Huu Ts'say turned away. "The clay I found was not good. My man wanted me to hurry for his hunting was more important than my looking for clay. We hardly have any meat left and the winter is not here." Huu Ts'say turned her head away fighting back her tears.

The other sisters clicked their tongues. "You do not have to tell us of your troubles, we have our own. Men are busy with their lives but we have our own fears, too. Here we are, all of us except for Munu, waiting for our children to be born and we have no food to last us through the winter. We cannot think bad thoughts or our times will get worse."

Munu's sisters were busy with their talk, however, they were now going to take Huu Ts'say home to rest. The soft evening breeze reminded her of the duty to her family. Munu took off her apron and hurried home. Her father and mother met her ready to go to the forest, for the sun was now fading over the mountains. Munu led them to the forest path. She put her arm around the tall cottonwood tree trunk. "You cannot see him during the day. He is only here at night."

Mother came up to her, "Munu, what are you telling us? We wish you to have a good life and a home with many children. We do not want you to be an outcast with your people. You are not telling us all of your feelings about his man or who he is. Is he a spirit?"

Munu shook her head, "I do not know who he is. He is kind and he listens to me when I speak. His feelings and mine are good. I do not know what he does, but during the day he is a skull with fingers."

Father did not answer. Mother pulled Munu to her, "Call him out and let us meet him. Give us the right to know him."

Munu walked quietly to the bush she had found him near the day before. She called softly and the skull's fingers reached up out of the brush.

"You are not afraid of me?"

"No, I want you to meet my parents."

"Let us wait until dark."

The sun fell over the hills and a handsome man walked out of the bush. "Now, I am ready."

Mother cast her eyes down as he moved toward them. Father knew that this was great magic, his daughter was chosen by the spirits to be with this man. It was not for him to question why.

The marriage was agreed upon. It would be at night in the Pueblo, but not in the bright fires of the plaza. The skull man agreed not to see Munu until the night of their union. Mother and father walked back with Munu. Father took the women to their home, then went to speak with the Elders.

The Elders chanted to the Great-Up-Above Spirits for understanding, also for the prayer that if this was an evil spirit they would be strong enough to fitght against it.

Mother came with Munu to the marriage ceremony. The drums began to beat. A circle was formed around her, everyone was eager to see this man who would be her husband. The chanting continued. The handsome man did not come. Munu cast her eyes down trying not to let the tears show as she danced alone. The fires burned down, the wind blew gently and soon other moccasins joined hers in the circle. Her man had come to the Gwingwendi-e.

Her handsome man was there with his hair long to his waist, his white shirt showed off his dark face, his loin cloth and leggings were embroidered with blues and greens. He danced around her touching her arm, pulling on her belt, cat-calling as he turned. The others in the Pueblo laughed with him, he was fun. Everyone liked him by the time the dance was finished.

Mother and father met them after the dance giving them cornmeal, flour, pinon nuts and corn. Munu accepted these while her husband received a hunting knife, fox skins, and sharpened arrows. The two of them left before dawn.

Munu let her skull husband carry most of the items; she tucked the bedrolls and her personal things under her arms. As they walked to the spring a thought crossed her mind. Where was she going to stay. The skull husband lived in a bush during the day and at night he wandered about. She turned to ask him, but the sun was already up and her husband was not there. The bundles he was carrying were gone also.

"Husband, husband, where are you?" There was no answer. "Husband, where am I to stay?" There was only the soft wind to answer her. Munu put her things down. Should she go back to the Pueblo? Should she put her pride aside and go back? Her legs were tired, her back ached from all the dancing, her head was again filled with questions and there was no one to answer them.

Munu left her things in a pile and walked to the bush. "Husband, where are we to live?" The bush was quiet. Munu knelt down next to it, "Are you there, my husband? Where are we to live?" Silence filled her ears. Not even the birds were chirping. Munu felt deserted but her father had told her to believe. So, she must. She walked around the forest. The tall cottonwood trees were her only company. Munu walked up on the hill to a flowing spring. There were only some rabbits nibbling at the clover. She turned and spotted a ladder sticking up from the ground. It appeared to come out of a hole. Munu quietly walked over to it. She peered down the hole.

"Husband, are you in there?" Munu spoke more to herself than to the darkness in the hole.

"Yes, I am here. Bring your things down here."

Munu was relieved at her good fortune. She stumbled in her hurry to bring her things back to the ladder. She dropped them down the hole and followed. The hole was very dark and her eyes took a long while to adjust. The mud floor was sealed with goat's blood. There were animal skins of all kinds on the walls. Baskets filled with feathers covered the floor. In one of these baskets was the skull. Munu unrolled her things and placed them on the shelves. There were no cooking utensils. She would make do with what she could find or use from the forest.

"Do you eat?" she asked the skull.

"No, I never eat during the day and unless I move about a lot at night I am not usually hungry."

Munu frowned, "Then you are not a hunter?"

"No, I am not a hunter."

Munu counted the animal skins on the wall. "How did you get these?"

The skull said, "The skins that you see were put there by my father who thought he could free his people from hunger with skins. They did not want them. My father died and the skins are all I have left to remember him by."

Munu took off her manta, hanging it behind a blanket. Her cotton skirt and blouse were pulled on and her apron was wrapped around her waist. She came out to clean and prepare her new home.

"Did you know your mother?"

The skull was now quiet. The sun was high in the sky and the heat from the earth was warming up the underground home.

Munu sat next to the basket with the skull in it. He whispered out to her, "I cannot talk for very long when I am like this. The spirits made me this way to be silent and to listen, sometimes with the ears on my head and other times with the ears of my spirit. I have learned to be silent out of respect for Mother Earth and her animals. To kill without thought of what was killed is most disrespectful. Therefore, I am to be a skull at the time when most men are busy hunting. I learn by watching."

Munu studied her skull husband as he lay inside the dark basket. She reached out to touch the basket, it was soft, almost like woven hair. The color of the basket was the same color as her husband's hair at night. The feathers the skull was perched on were eagle feathers. Munu studied the skull, it did not move.

Munu made several trips to the spring for willows to weave mats to sleep on, tree bark for plates and cooking boards. Her day was filled with exploring her needs for their home and what was actually available to her. The skins loomed up at her each time she entered the underground room. They were dusty and old. The heads of the skins watched her every move. The clay for her pottery she dragged down last. The soft pelts that she used to hold the clay embarrassed her but she decided that she used them for a good practical purpose.

The soft light of evening fell across the ceiling from the hole above. Munu felt alone. Her sisters may have husbands that work them too hard, but at least they have husbands that are there most of the time. Munu gathered up the loose willows and tied the bundle together. She swept up the floor of the home that was now hers. The dust flew, her eyes teared, she was tired. She had settled into her new home by herself, for herself, to live with a man who was only partially there.

Birds hopped near the ladder chirping and flittering. Munu gathered up some cornmeal and threw it up to them. They danced around it pecking away with delight. Children would be another consideration in her life. What would she do if her children were to be born like their father? Enough of this, thought Munu. She had made a decision in her life and she would make it work for her. She was strong and brave. This life she had chosen would be a good one, she would see to it. The sun rolled over to land on the horizon. Munu climbed the ladder to see the red purple sunset color of the clouds on the horizon. The colors were magnificent. Father Sun certainly must believe in the way of the spirits or he would not show off so much beauty.

Munu climbed back down the ladder. She leaned against the warm wall letting her thoughts rest. She let her eyes close. A hand rubbed her back. She quickly awoke. The home was dark, pitch black. She squinted to see who was next to her but could not make out a shadow.

"It is I, your husband, Munu, would you like to go with me to the spring?"

Munu felt along the floor to her bedroll. "No, I can't, I am very tired. Let me sleep for awhile, then wake me before the sun rises." She curled up on her bedroll and fell asleep.

The days turned into months. Munu changed her lifestyle to be awake during the night and to sleep in the day. There were times when she had to go into the Pueblo for social engagements or to trade her pottery for supplies. The skull husband had no trade that she knew of to help out in supporting them.

She had not desired children, for the teasing she got in the Pueblo would be mean to inflict on children. Women her age laughed at her, her friends from before would call her the skull's wife. They would ask her if she had any bones for children yet. Her father had become a recluse for the jokes made about his skull son were more than he could take. Munu's mother laughed with the people, then later she would tell Munu, "They are afraid of your skull husband and so they must make jokes and laugh at what they do not understand. There is a lot of fear also for the people are hungry and winter approaches with no food in our storage rooms."

Snow fell and with it the fear of starvation. The people were searching for wood, berries, and any little animal they could find that would make a meal. The nights were too cold now for crops to grow and the lack of rain hadn't given much yield to the harvest of the fall. The men had no supplies of jerky so they could not go very far from the Pueblo to hunt.

Father came one night to Munu's home. He was very solemn through the meal. After the meal he turned to the skull husband, "Do you think you could help us? You have told Munu that your father was a great hunter of animal skins. You have many on the wall. Could we borrow them for warmth when we go out for the hunt?"

Skull husband thought on this very carefully. "You want to borrow the skins to trick the animals that you are hunting, also to keep the hunters warm, isn't that right?"

Father's face warmed into a smile. Skull husband continued, "Then you may take them, but on one condition; you let me join the hunting party."

Father's smile changed to a frown. "You cannot go hunting with us. We hunt during the day and you are only a man at night."

Skull husband shook his head. "Then if I cannot come, you cannot use my skins." Father agreed to let skull husband come with them on the hunt.

At sun up the next day the skull husband turned into a skull. He had told father to place him hear the gorge where the animals used to run down the mountain. Father walked along the path until he came to a tall ponderosa pine tree. There was a low, forgotten, dark brown, dried branch bending over the path. Father held skull husband high over his head. Skull husband reached up with his delicate bony fingers grabbing hold of the bark. He pulled himself up balancing on the dried branch. Father left him.

Skull husband listened for the animals. All he heard was the early morning breeze filtering through the trees. PLOP! Something landed on top of skull husband. It dripped down his cheek. PLOP! More sap dripped from above. He listened and heard hooves clicking against rocks. The sound was coming closer. A bird of great strength flew up to a branch over skull husband and dropped a feather of many colors. As it floated down past him the colors faded, reappearing on the white, sticky skull.

An elk ran with great speed straight towards skull husband. Skull husband held firmly to the dried branch with his bony fingers, swinging down into the path of the elk. The leading elk froze at the sight of him. Skull husband called all the powers of his family within him, chanting:

"Let me be the warrior of the Rainbow
Let me bring food to those who are dying
Let the colors of my face bring thanks for this meat
Food for the people to grow and be strong
So that they may be kind and give thanks."

The first ten elk fell where they stood. This frightened off the other elk which bounded away out of sight. The hunters crept through the gorge. They came upon the ten elk lying dead on the path. They were not wounded, nor did they suffer in any way, there were no marks on them. They were just dead.

Father crept over to skull husband. "What happened to the elk?" Skull husband whispered, "They died for a purpose."

The other hunters cheered with delight. The hunters hung the elk on their carrying sticks. Father carried the mulit-colored skull husband back to the Pueblo. They agreed to have a feast in the night to celebrate the greatest hunter in the Pueblo. The skull husband could hunt without spear or bow, a hunter who killed for a purpose, without causing pain.

The hunters gave him the name Soetuwa Ts'aa. The elk meat fed the people until the cold spell passed. Munu was now regarded with respect and father had a new story to boast about with the Elders.

Skull husband and Munu had three normal children. The fourth child she gave birth to was a skull with long thin arms. He stayed in the underground home. No one spoke about him until skull husband had taught him how to hunt in the ways of magic. Then he, too, became a hunter in his own right and was given the name Muuyo' Sen Ts'aa.

"All of this has made me very hungry. While I fix dinner you clean up the floor. We must rest for awhile. There have been too many stories and too much work." Grandfather left me to my thoughts.

The world had turned white by morning. All the trees were white bony fingers of ice. Whipped cream ground moved up to the windows of white. The dogs yelped in the back yard. Leroy must have brought them back early.

Grandfather was drinking hot coffee in the kitchen, reading a note. "Hello, did you sleep well?" I nodded, my voice was not awake yet. "Leroy took the dogs to the vet. Cost seventy-eight dollars to get those mutts shot full of stuff. I'll have to put them to work."

The coffee was strong, it warmed my soul. The willows were soft, pliable and ready for weaving. We worked for several hours without much to say. The dogs had been fed and they were making most of the noise barking at everything and anyone that went by the house.

"Grandfather, I have a story that someone told me. The translation is not very good, maybe if I tell it you could help explain it to me."

"Maybe."

"Would you like to hear it?"

"I'm listening, aren't I?"

6

KAY-SEN D'OH

Janini-povi was a wise young medicine man with great powers in magic. Junse-Anu was his woman and she also was knowledgeable in the same, and that is how their marriage came about. Janini-povi told this story while they were walking in a forest during the time of the Paayogedi.

"When I was very young, five or six years of age, my mother and father became very ill with a fever from the spirits. I was sent out by my oldest aunt to pick pinon nuts for a stew. This was of great importance to me for I felt that the pinon nuts would save my mother and father from harm.

I started back to the Pueblo before the tssawa of evening with my pouch of pinon. The path was well worn back to the Pueblo — I knew I could not get lost. The turn in the path that led to the flatlands of the Pueblo was blocked by a Kay-Sen D'oh, a large white bear. The Kay-Sen D'oh appeared to be sleeping. I looked for another way to go around the bear. I was raised to have great respect for grandfather bear.

To the left of the bear was a very thick bramble of wild plum bushes. To the right of the bear was a thick long line of cactus. There was no short cut home around this Kay-Sen D'oh. I could go all the way back and find my own path to the Pueblo, but then I could get lost and come home in the dark, too late to give the precious pinon to my sick parents.

The easiest solution was to go over or under the white bear. I was old enough to know that grandfather bear, when angered, could hurt or kill. This Kay-Sen D'oh had soft fluffy fur and I was confident he would not hurt me. I decided to go over the bear. I came up very close to him and could see him breathing, his nose large and moist. His mouth was slightly open and his tongue was hanging down to the side. I reached out and touched the Kay-Sen D'oh. I stroked his big, white, furry paw. He didn't move, I continued to stroke him, not believing my luck and liking the feel of his soft fur. He still didn't move. My courage increased. I knew that I could crawl over his neck, which was the thinnest part of his body, and run home with the pinon and a good story.

I put the pouch around my back, leaned forward and gently touched a roll of furry fat that hung down from his chin. I grasped it tenderly with my hands and started to pull myself over his body.

My strong grasp was almost knocked loose when the Kay-Sen D'oh stood up growling, holding me in his large, rough padded paws. His hot, thick breath blew into my face. I did not scream or cry out because I was a brave boy and did not want the bear to know I was afraid. 'Yugeh Janini-Povi' became my name. A stillness filled my body. I opened my eyes very wide and stared at the bear. The bear's little brown-silver eyes stared back at me. The bear's paws loosened their grip. I hugged the thick rolls of fat firmly for the bear was standing upright and I was a great distance from the ground. I let him carry me while I hung onto his thick furry neck. I lay my head against his big shoulder and watched the path to my Pueblo move farther and farther away from me. I held firmly to the Kay-Sen D'oh with my fingers burning.

Soon we came to a cave. The cave was frightening. Father taught me that it was dangerous to enter a cave if there was a bear near by. The real danger was being caught between a mother bear and cubs. I had not taken notice if this was a mother bear or not.

I had no choice but to be carried into the cave by the Kay-Sen D-oh. There were no cubs in the cave. The bear and I were the only ones there. It was a very dark cave. Slowly my eyes were able to focus on what was around me. On the cave walls were bows and arrows, baskets, dolls and drawn masks.

On the floor under this wall were bowls of khowa ts'say, khuu kaay and khuu oyegi mixed with khuu kw'a'aa'i. This gave me the thought that there was a person who lived with this bear and worked with corn magic. A calm came over me.

Grumbling and knocking noises came from the back of the cave. It was too dark to see what the bear was doing, but it soon came out holding a leather pouch in its mouth. The pouch was dropped in front of me. I opened it to find bread, white cheese, dried fruit and shelled nuts. Hunger had taken over my body without my knowing it. With great appreciation I ate my fill only taking some of each food. The leftover food I laid out on the cave floor for the Kay-Sen D'oh. The bear cupped the food in his paws and licked it up. This was most unusual for the bears near the Pueblo only ate berries and fruit; perhaps on occasion they would go into farmers' gardens after melons, but never did I know of a bear that ate bread.

Sleep overtook my body as night came upon us. I awoke in the morning to a big fire at the mouth of the cave. At first the fire appeared to be out of control; then I saw the white bear. He came walking past me from the back of the cave holding a log in his mouth. He dropped the log on the fire and walked away shaking the ash off his furry, white head.

He nuzzled me with his nose. The bear had carried me to his cave, fed me, kept me warm, and now was playing with me. All my fear gone, I hugged the bear back, patting his soft white rolls of fur. Kay-Sen D'oh fell down next to me and started patting me with his fat long-clawed paws.

I stared at his silver-brown eyes and felt brave enough to speak, "Great white bear, why am I here?"

The bear grumbled in his throat, the noise rising to the surface came out in words. "I must be truthful with you, you are here for a reason." His voice startled me and I withdrew my hand. He sat up on his thick legs, white fur rolled over his hind haunches.

"When you return to your Pueblo, Janini-Povi, your family will be dead. Many people you know will be dead. I had to take you away from the Pueblo before you got the fever and your death would be the end of your family's wisdom. I brought you here — it is safe, you will not get sick. I brought you here to teach you the ways of medicine."

I knew that this was very important and I should listen and learn with great seriousness. I was there for a purpose.

I stayed with the Kay-Sen D'oh for many years. We gathered food, willow withes from the river and fish from the small streams. We had everything we needed in the cave. As I got older, he allowed me into the back of the cave. There were large grain pots in the back that were made from thick coils of clay which had been pushed together with a thumbnail. Each one of these large grain pots held a different color cornmeal. The Kay-Sen D'oh shared his knowledge with me when I questioned him. He explained that one pot held birth, another honesty, and another honor and pride, each a treasure for man. The great white bear explained to me that no one was to ever have the big grain pots and when I was older I would understand why.

Later one cold winter night when the fire burned low, I got up to put a log on the fire. I noticed that one of the grain pots was missing along with Kay-Sen D'oh. I never questioned him on this for this was the great white bear's purpose and I was separate.

When I was fourteen, I heard people shouting and calling out to one another while they were picking pinon nuts. The bear was out of the cave so I decided to go down and find out if any of the people knew of my family. As I started out of the cave a very tall man met me. He had long white hair braided down his back to his knees. His eyes were silver-brown and he had a leather kilt around his middle, on his chest were bear claws hanging from a leather thong.

When he touched me I knew who he was, he was Kay-Sen D'oh. He took me back inside the cave. He lifted a hollowed out bear fetish and filled it with cornmeal. He sealed it with berry sap and handed it to me.

He stared into my eyes for a long time telling me things I couldn't hear. Then we turned and walked out of the cave down to the people. That is where I live now and those are the people I live with, the people of our Pueblo.

I never saw him again and all the times I have gone back to find the cave — there is no cave. I cannot find a cave at all."

Junse-Anu asked, "So you learned your magical powers from the great white bear?"

"Yes, he was my family and my father. I miss him at times greatly — yet I know he is watching and he will always be with me."

———————————

Grandfather cleared his throat, "You told that story very well. Where did you hear it?"

I pushed my hair back from my face. "I learned it from Uncle Tito."

Grandfather pulled out a cigar. "You are wise to listen and remember, the stories are too important to be forgotten or lost. Your story reminds me of a story my mother told. Hand me those willows from the silver bucket and I will tell it to you."

"But Grandfather, what does the story I told mean?"

"That is up to you. Now listen."

7

SIBO'PENE

Once in the other Pueblo, the one up higher on the mountain, there was a terrible drought that came upon the land, the worst drought anyone could remember. Everyone felt this was a time of dissatisfaction with the spirits.

The drought came slowly at first. Rain would appear on the horizon only to be blown away by the wind in the night, leaving Sun to heat the land, wilting the plants that were unable to sustain life through another hard, hot day. Wind would come up as a light breeze, then by midday the wind would rage through the dried plants crinkling whatever might have been saved to powder.

Thus, the testing time came to the people. The heat of the day would rise as the days moved further into the times of distrust. People started to steal from their families, others would hide what they had and would not share. The children, the Elders, the animals all licked cracked lips in the dirt blown fields.

Each clan gathered together to rethink their approach. The women worked on their own version in solving this problem. The people continued to find fault and blame each other even though they knew they were being tested. The anger and hostility that had brought them to this point in the testing was hard to give up and not easily forgotten.

An Elder from the Fish Clan, Kwahtaa, came into the kiva. The others were hungry, thirsty and tired. Kwahtaa listened to the Elders talk about the food shortage, the lack of water and the river which now ran as a small stream filled with rotting dead fish.

Kwahtaa stood up and nodded to the oldest Elder. "I have come from the edge of the forest. There on the side of a small hill is a spring with fresh flowing water."

The old Elder studied him. Kwahtaa was a grandfather; he had many children, grandchildren, and was known for his wisdom. Kwahtaa had also been known for his greed. There were times when he could have shared, but didn't, Kwahtaa had only respect to gain now.

"Kwahtaa, will you lead us to this spring? For this would be a great honor if indeed you were the one to find a way to save our people and our Pueblo."

"Yes, I will lead you, let us go now." Kwahtaa let the other more respectable Elders go up the ladder before him. He then walked ahead of the others to the forest. In his mind, Kwahtaa could see the spring. He would show them this spring that still flowed with good clean water. Kwahtaa led them through the forest, the needles from the pine trees lying in thick abundance on the ground. The needles remaining on the trees were yellow and dry in the hot air of the midday swelter. The others followed, ready to believe, for they were a desperate group. The spring they were led to was not running. In fact, it was nothing more than a dry little gully runoff from a time when the heavy rains did cause water to run off down the hill. Kwahtaa was surprised with honest emotion that the other Elders respected him. They believed he really thought he saw a spring. His disappointment was real.

Kwahtaa's vision brought him prestige and the Elders believed his clan should be the first to chant to the spirits for understanding. The Fish Clan gathered in the kiva with their bellies full of what food they could get to help them through the many days of chanting. No one thought the chanting would last too long, surely the rains would come before they would all become hungry again. They chanted for days, more days, many, many days, until they were all so weak they could not stand. Their lips were parched, their bellies swollen from lack of food, and their minds losing the ability to think.

The wood they used to burn the fires in the kiva was brought by a young boy whose sister was a student of an Elder in the Fish Clan. They asked the boy to get his sister and tell her to come with her baskets filled with water. This was not usually allowed, but since the occasion was not a usual one the boy ran off to get his sister. She returned bringing the water and also some dried meat. The Elders rationed the food and drank the water sparingly.

The Elders were cautious for they were uncertain of the spirits' approval of such food and water during the time of testing. Soon the food ran out, and at last after many days the water was gone. They called up to the boy and told him the next day they would need more food and water. It was agreed they should fast one day more before getting more food and water.

Kwahtaa sat chanting with the others. He thought of his family, his children, his grandchildren and his fields. Would he ever see them again? Kwahtaa had a good life before the testing came. He had been a man of power and prestige. He had always eaten well and so had his family. This fasting was not something he was accustomed to, he wanted to eat and drink, drink from the spring with the cool water pouring out onto the hot ground.

Kwahtaa envisioned the flowing spring and kept thinking of it over and over again. His lips were chapped from the dry hot air in the kiva. His eyes burned with the dust that floated through the kiva every time someone moved. It had become difficult for him to swallow. That night the Elder sat leaning against the banco. Kwahtaa watched the other Elders fall asleep. He sat there and in his mind could hear the water of the spring gurgling, running, flowing, cool and moist. The spring was calling to him. It was not meant for the others. Kwahtaa studied the other Elders around him. They were all in a deep sleep. The night air was hot, sweat dripped down Kwahtaa's face as he planned his escape. He counted out the approximate steps it would take for him to get to the ladder. The ladder had twelve bars across it. The fourth one from the top squeaked when full weight was put on it. The step at the top would put him in full view of anyone walking around the Pueblo or someone looking out of a doorway. He would have to sprint across the plaza to the side entrance, then he would be able to run to the spring. Kwahtaa examined each Elder with his eyes. They were not moving. Kwahtaa took his counted steps across the kiva to the ladder. He climbed up the ladder quietly to the top. Carefully moving over the fourth bar on the ladder, he could see the plaza clearly. The stars were bright. No one was up and no one was outside. He kept low to the ground to avoid being seen.

Kwahtaa hurried out of the plaza to the road. He ran with as much speed as he could to the spring. The water flowed, the water gurgled up and out of the hole in the earth. Kwahtaa fell on his knees. He cupped his hands and drank of the water. He splashed the water on his face, and poured it over his head. Then he pulled off his ceremonial shirt and rubbed the water on his chest. His hands started to shake, his eyes started to tear, he was weak. He fell into the water.

The water rolled into his mouth flowing over his face. Water washed his tired eyes, flowed into his ears and rinsed the dirt out of his long hair. The water gurgled around his chest and arms. The cool, wet, smooth water washed the dirt off his body, moistened his lips and cooled his burning eyes. Kwahtaa rolled over and over and over in the spring water. Then he lay with his head staring up at the stars. The water flowed over his body rocking him easily into a deep sleep. His body, cold and wet did not wake him.

The birds came and chirped near him, the rabbits hopped by, cautious of any movement. Finally the sun's rays hit Kwahtaa's face. He woke up with a start. Daylight was here. Kwahtaa quickly gathered up his long hair, rolling it back up into a chongo. He frantically searched for his ceremonial shirt. He could not find it. In a state of panic he hunted for it in the forest, then the sunlight reflected something shiny in the water. He ran to it and pulled up his shirt, wet all the way through. He pulled the embroidered leather shirt over his head. It would not come down over his shoulders. He danced around tugging at the shirt, pulling on it, tearing it in places, and finally got it over his head, his arms through the armholes. The feathers and beads that decorated his ceremonial shirt were all over him and the ground. Kwahtaa now had to re-roll his hair. He did this as he walked quickly to the kiva.

The plaza was busy with people. They all walked out into the field at one point. The children were given orders of some kind. Kwahtaa hurried to the ladder. He cautiously listened for chanting, there was none. He lifted his foot onto the first bar of the ladder. Then he put his foot on the second bar, there were no voices. Kwahtaa smiled to himself, the others were still asleep. He then lowered himself to the third bar. No response. Then the fourth and weakest bar of the ladder was reached. The bar of the ladder squeaked loudly. Kwahtaa ducked his head under and peered around him. Some of the Elders were watching him. Others were still asleep in the corner. Kwahtaa opened his mouth to speak, but instead of words water flowed out of his mouth. He turned his eyes upward to the sky and water burst forth out of his eye sockets, pouring water all over him. Then his ears burst forth with water streaming down the sides of his body. At this he went limp, his limbs broke from his body, and water gushed into the kiva. The other Elders cried out in surprise when the water poured onto them.

Once the water hit the floor of the kiva some of the Elders were turned into fish. The Elder in the corner tried to jump up away from the water but he was quickly swept up and turned into a turtle. The thin Elder, who had come into the Fish clan in the summer, turned into a water snake, and some others were turned into frogs. This happened very quickly before any of the cries could be heard. At midday the girl came to bring more dried fish to the Elders. She noticed that the fire was out so she went back to her home and gathered some twigs for the Elders' fire in the kiva. When she returned she heard a strange sound. Thinking nothing of it, she stepped on the first bar of the ladder. No one called up to her, so she continued down the ladder. On the fourth bar of the ladder she turned very slowly and looked down. All she saw was water slowly rising higher and higher. In fear she dropped her basket of fish and fled out of the kiva. The water surged upward with a tremendous force when the basket hit. Water shot straight up into the air lifting the roof off the kiva. The fourteen-year-old girl ran to the Pueblo.

The girl ran to the first home near the plaza. She knocked and knocked on the door. No one answered. "Help, help, please answer me." The girl ran to the second home. She pounded on the wooden frame calling out, "Help, there is something terribly wrong, help." No one came to the door. The girl ran to the third door frame. She screamed out, "Ai-e, ai-e." She ran to the fourth home.

As she lifted her hand to knock on the door frame an old grandfather grabbed her and pulled her into his home. "What is it? What has happened with the chanting at the kiva?"

"The Elders are all gone, the kiva was full of water when I went down. I dropped my basket and water rose over the kiva taking off the roof and now water is flowing all over and it is rising."

The grandfather grabbed some dried corn from a viga. "Here, take this and run, run to the high road. Get the Elders from the Pueblo up north. The testing has ended, someone did an evil selfish deed. You must run and save what we have left. Go." He pushed the girl out of the doorway. Water was moving steadily towards them, gaining height and speed.

The girl ran to the top of the road, then turned and looked back. All she saw was a high wall of water moving towards her. The girl turned and ran until her feet ached from the sharp stones that cut through her moccasins on the cross-country path. She tried hard to breathe, but her chest burned in pain from the struggle to keep going. Tears washed down her face mixing with the dirt. The girl stopped quickly and turned, the wall of water was following her. The Pueblo she had left behind was completely gone. All that remained was a tremendous body of water carrying with it feathers, baskets, rugs and debris. Crying children's voices echoed through the water's rushing sounds.

The girl ran on and on to the high land. The water followed her. At last she found the high road, the worn path from her Pueblo to another. She slacked off on her fast run because she knew now she was close to help. She turned, watching the water behind her, and lost her footing. She fell back, hugged the corn to her chest and with the other hand braced herself. She pushed her legs under her to get up, but she couldn't find the strength.

Father Sky watched from above, Mother Earth let the roaring water gain speed. Wind blew around the sacred corn in the girl's hands. The girl struggled, then she lay back. The water moved on at its fast pace, high and deadly it moved swiftly over her leaving her a statue of rock.

Grandfather handed me a finished basket. The colors mixed together to make an intricate pattern. "It is done. Get your things, I will take you home." I did as I was told.

Grandfather pulled the truck out of the driveway. His finished basket sat next to me on the seat. "So, you heard a lot of stories and now you think you have helped your grandfather?"

I watched the road. "You haven't helped your grandfather." The truck bumped over the corrugated wash that was called the county road. "You haven't told me anything I don't already know."

Grandfather pulled down the sun visor. "Well, are you going to tell me something I don't know or what?" I frowned. He did this every time.

"I feed you and care for you and you won't leave me anything to remember this trip." Grandfather was feeling lonely already. He did need something to tell the widow.

I stopped him before he could continue, "Yes, I can tell you something you may not know."

This time he watched me out of the corner of his eye. I sucked in some fresh crisp air and began my story.

8

CARETAKER CATS

Far to the south of here was a Pueblo badly in need of direction. The people worked hard and appreciated the rewards from their hard work, but they needed direction. There were large animals that lived with these people and guided them when it was time to plant or harvest or give thanks. The large animals had grown very fond of the people but they felt the cause they were born for was being put aside by the demands of the people in this particular Pueblo.

One night the animals met in the kiva and decided they would leave regardless of the people's needs. They would go their own ways to lead their own lives.

One animal with common sense interrupted them, "We cannot go away after all these years and expect the people to know what they are doing. Someone should stay here."

All the animals stopped to think this over. The Bobcat sniffed his nose, the Wolf licked his thick lips, the Coyote giggled, the Small Black Bear leaned back closing his eyes.

"Well then, who shall stay?" No one wanted to be chosen or picked. They had all worked very hard and all wanted their freedom from this overwhelming responsibility.

The Mountain Lion leaned forward and scratched, pulling out a flat pack of rolling paper, some tobacco and a flint. He rolled himself a cigarette, then passed the papers and tobacco around.

The Mountain Lion wiped his whiskers, "The people need a cat of some kind." This made all the other cats nervous. Mountain Lion stood, "Let me think for awhile, I bet I can remember an old trick."

The animals puffed, some staring off into space, others preoccupied with their neighbor's smoke.

Mountain Lion walked to the middle of the kiva, "I am ready." He lifted his furry head and sneezed a most powerful sneeze. A small female cat flew out of his right nostril and landed on the mud floor. The Mountain Lion sniffed, then let out another great sneeze. Another cat, a male cat, came out of his left nostril. These two cats shook themselves off and started to clean.

"Smart animals, they are cleaning up first." The Bear was impressed. The Wolf was very distrustful and the Coyote sat with a gleeful smile on his face.

The Mountain Lion started to sneeze again and again. He was overcome with sneezes. The kiva quickly filled with cats all washing themselves and eyeing each other.

The Bobcat was the first one to the ladder, the others followed. The Mountain Lion was the last to leave, "You are my offspring, you have my whiskers, my face and my hunting abilities. When you have little cats the people will be overjoyed at their cute, furry smallness and they will want them. In gratitude for the people's kindnesses to you, you will hunt and kill their mice. At night you tell them the way of wisdom and keep them in line. You cats watch out for these people." The Mountain Lion hurried up the ladder to join his friends who had already disappeared into the dark night.

Grandfather smiled, "Uncle Tito did not tell you that story." I kept my vision on the snowy road. The truck rattled. Grandfather patted my knee.

"That was one story you have told me that I know for a fact was not from Uncle Tito." When we arrived at my home, he let me off at the driveway.

"Thank you, Nee-nee, for the compliment." I nodded and gave him a hug. After all, that story came from the best storyteller I know — how could I resist.

That night as I lay in my own bed, the sky outside was filled with stars. There was an emptiness inside me, a feeling of longing. "Great Ones, why is it I love the people of the Pueblo proudly, but I can never be one of them? Their stories come from the soul and reflect the faith you have had in them. Now, I live in town with people that have their own ways that are foreign to me." The quilt on my bed was warm, I pulled it back and went to the window.

"I do not know these people in town. Their ways are so different from mine, their life is a faster pace, their vision of distance is hurried by time. I miss the Pueblo, I miss the people I grew up with, but when I go back to the Pueblo everything is changed. The good warmth of my friends is different. Where do I belong?"

The wind blew gently as if in answer. I closed my eyes. The night sky covered the land from the town to the Pueblo. Somewhere there was a girl like me who grew up with a family she loved, someone who was transplanted from one culture to another. This child, like me, would know of her family traditions but remain an outsider, not to be totally accepted into the culture of her parents' choosing. There was a richness to being in both and knowing both cultures, yet it left a feeling of incompleteness.

I opened the window. "Strength, strength, believe in ourselves, do not seek approval from others that you love." Where did those words come from?

The Pueblo was a land I could never go back to with the same feelings of security that I had when my parents had the Mercantile. Now, it was time for me to learn the ways of those around me and to accept them. I climbed back into bed. "Give me a story to sleep with, give me a story of long ago to remember, for I hurt, I hurt way down deep." The wind blew against my window making a soft purring sound. My thoughts of loneliness disappeared.

9

BROTHER WHITE MOON

"Moon Sister, Moon Sister, wake up, wake," the bright colored twin cried out in the night. Moon Sister stirred her yellow hue from deep slumber. "Look, Moon Sister, it is Kunt-a woh-hah, he is back roaming Mother Earth again."

The Moon Sister smiled. "I will stop him this time. He is mine, you went last time and failed, I will bring him back this time."

Moon Sister let herself fall down to Mother Earth. Kunt-a woh-hah whizzed along the surface of Mother Earth scaring animals to death. Children dropped in their tracks, wind ran through the trees and Kunt-a woh-hah laughed.

Moon Sister let herself fall closer to him, she changed her appearance into that of a beautiful woman. Kunt-a woh-hah heard her laughter and turned to frighten her. Moon Sister closed her eyes. She smiled a rich warm smile. Kunt-a woh-hah hurdled full force towards her, Moon Sister let him pass right through her illusion. Kunt-a woh-hah was no longer laughing. He gritted his teeth and flung himself at her. Moon Sister kept her eyes shut and let him pass through her once again. She lifted off the ground calling him back. Kunt-a woh-hah flew around the bend in the canyon. The high sandstone walls hid him from her view. He peered around the bend over a chamisa bush.

The beautiful maiden turned into a gorgeous buoyant bufferfly. Kunt-a woh-hah let the butterfly float around the sagebrush on the canyon walls, then he blinked. The butterfly grew into a dancing bird singing a sweet melody. The bird twirled in the clouds over his head. The bird was searching for him. Kunt-a woh-hah sommersaulted over the chamisa bush and came floating down to earth as a crisp brown cottonwood leaf. The bird caught sight of the leaf and tumbled after it. As the bird tumbled, it turned back into Moon Sister. She lifted the brown crisp leaf.

"Oh, you poor leaf, it is but spring and you have already lost your will to live. I will blow on you and give you some of my strength to grow green again."

Moon Sister blew her magic on the leaf, opening her path of strength to Kunt-a woh-hah. He reached into her breath and pulled all the magical life out of her. There is no more Moon Sister in the sky. She rides the waves of the rivers, the crests of the lakes and waits for Kunt-a woh-hah to return her magic. But Kunt-a woh-hah will not return to her for he is now so filled with magic that he is buried deep in the folds of Mother Earth.

Moon Sister shines up to her brother reflecting her love to him in the silver moving water.

Brother Moon cried tears of sorrow at the sight of Moon Sister's downfall. He decided he would do something of genuine goodness for a person on Mother Earth who also felt the loneliness and sorrow. Moon Brother shone over the creases of Mother Earth and found an old man and his woman who lived alone in a cliff dwelling far from others. They had dreamed of children and had none. They dreamed of being accepted by the cliff dwellers on the other river path but they were not, for the old man was too old to be of use to them. Moon Brother put his plan to work.

The old man lifted up off his bedroll and listened, his head cocked towards the door. His woman was snoring lightly next to him. The old man heard his name being called, "Tenyo, Tenyo, Tenyo." He sat upright. His moccasins were in his hand. The firelight had gone out hours ago, the night was still black. The sound outside stopped, Tenyo listened. Noiselessly he went to the door opening. There were two footprints left in the soft sand. They were fresh, made by someone heavy with large feet, no moccasins.

Tenyo let the door blanket fall behind him. He bent down low and followed the prints down the cliff dwelling path to the lowlands. The lowlands were not safe by daylight and at night it was known that spirits of all kinds roamed freely with no mercy.

Tenyo stopped, the path back up the cliff was close by, he could yet go back the way he had come. "Tenyo, Tenyo." The soft whisper reached his ears. Tenyo followed. The prints were harder to follow now for the high walls of the canyon blocked the light of the moon. Tenyo cautiously studied the ground in front of him. He knelt on one knee. A flash of light flew over his head; he did not see it. Tenyo stood and continued; his mind was preoccupied with the calling of his name. The wind blew his long white hair hard against his face. Tenyo fell back pushing his hair away from his eyes. As he fell another stream of light darted past him. Again, he did not see it. Tenyo grabbed at the dirt trying to get up, his hand touched a rock, a smooth rock. Tenyo pulled it to his side. He studied it with his fingers and his eyes. It was not a rock he had seen before, he tried to lift it to his lap, but it would not leave the ground. Tenyo pushed hard against it trying to lift himself to a standing position. He could not get up. He lifted his hand from the rock and the rock clung to his palm. Tenyo turned his hand and a grating noise behind him frightened him into dropping the rock.

"Who is there?" he whispered out into the darkness. A rustling sound moved towards him. Tenyo turned, there standing behind him were four large black bears. They stood on their hind feet with necklaces of pine braided around their necks. They were studying him.

"Tenyo?" He nodded. They waved their paws for him to follow them. They walked through the night to a place that was a mountain of rocks. From the top of the rocks smoke gathered in a circle, then rose to the sky. "Come." The four bears walked ahead into the rocks. Tenyo followed. The rock wall appeared to be solid, the bears moved through it, Tenyo did the same.

Women's voices wailed through the hollows of the rocks. Tenyo hurried to catch up with the four bears. He felt fear enter his soul. The women were wailing louder and louder all around him. Their voices were of great sorrow. the voices were right in front of him, but instead of women a great web of spiders hung down from the ceiling of the pathway. There came now another kind of wailing. A young boy's voice crying out in pain.

Tenyo turned to go away from the crying; he hit solid rock through which he could not pass. Tenyo turned back to return in the direction from which he had come, the rock closed around him. He resigned himself to move forward. The bears beckoned him to follow. Two bears went in one direction of the path, the others turned to go another way. Tenyo stopped. The crying was louder. Tenyo went with the bears who were in the pathway going away from the sound of crying. The two bears moved much faster than the old man. Tenyo soon grew tired and wanted to stop. The bears nodded. They sat down leaning back against the rocks. They closed their eyes, Tenyo did the same. Light trickled across his face. He opened his eyes fully expecting to be in his cliff dwelling. There in front of him was a large pillar of wood and at the top was a young boy crying out, "Tenyo, Tenyo, Tenyo, help me."

Tenyo stood and stared up. "Tenyo, Tenyo, help me." The voice was desperate.

Tenyo called up, "Who are you?"

The reply was the same, "Tenyo, help me."

Tenyo rubbed his hands together. There was no way he could climb up the pillar. His legs were tired, his hands calloused and old. Tenyo walked around the pillar. There was no rope that he could use, no long wooden sticks he could toss up to the boy. Tenyo sat down leaning against the wooden pillar.

Two small mice scurried around him. Tenyo watched them. The mice ran around him squeaking, oblivious to his presence. Tenyo watched, then with a movement so swift he himself could not explain, he caught a mouse. He tied it firmly with a leather thong from his moccasin. He took the mouse outside the cave. The sun shone brightly. Tenyo studied the sky. Two large eagles swooped through the air playing. Tenyo took his mouse and went to the top of a canyon. He dug a hole through the limestone. The hole was very deep. He crawled into it. Then he held the mouse in his hand up out of the hole opening. He waited. The mouse wriggled and squeaked. The eagles dove in the hot sun searching for food. Tenyo waited. A talon landed on his hand grabbing and pecking at the mouse. Tenyo, with greater speed than before, captured the eagle letting the mouse run free across the sand. The eagle's sharp beak stabbed at his hand. Tneyo took his shirt, threw it over his head onto the eagle. The eagle was quiet and rigid in his hand. Tenyo took the eagle with him into the cave. The boy was crying quietly now. His tears fell from above landing on Tenyo's hand.

Tenyo held the eagle firmly. He then began to chant. He danced around the wooden pillar twirling with each chorus of his song. The eagle relaxed with the chant and the swaying movement of the dance. Tenyo danced, twirled, and chanted until the sun was over the edge of the earth. Then Tenyo removed his cloth shirt from the eagle's body. The eagle tensed.

"Eagle, you know that I will not harm you, I will give you your freedom if you will give the boy his freedom." Tenyo let the eagle go. The eagle soared up to the boy, he grabbed the leather rope that tied the boy and lifted it up to the roof of the cave. Then the eagle was gone.

The rope fell at Tenyo's feet. The boy cried, "Tenyo, Tenyo, help me get down." Tenyo leaned back against the pillar. The night was still, the wind was gentle. Tenyo closed his eyes. Brother Moon shone through the opening of the cave. Small night creatures crawled in and out of the door opening. Tenyo watched a lizard with no eyes slither up the rock wall. Another small snake slithered through the night and hurried to a shadow waiting for a meal to come. Tenyo thought.

74

The lizard crawled up the rock moving towards him. Tenyo lifted his hand from his side and with the swfitness of a snake gathered up the lizard. Tenyo held him carefully until dawn. Then Tenyo started his dance once more. He danced until midday. Then he told the lizard, "I am not going to hurt you. Climb up the pillar of wood and give the rope to the boy."

He tied the rope around the lizard's tail placing him on the wooden pillar. The lizard climbed up the pillar to the boy. He gave him the rope and was gone. The boy grabbed at the rope. "Tenyo, help me, I am too weak to hold myself on this rope, I cannot get down." Tenyo walked to the cave opening. He watched deer and elk run past the cave. Tenyo tied his moccasin tightly and ran with great swiftness after a small elk. He ran with the wind. The elk fell in a hole and lay calling to its mother. Tenyo caught the elk, lifted it up off the ground and carried it to the cave. Tenyo felt the heart beat of the small elk. He saw the fear of death in its eyes. Tenyo placed the elk at the base of the wooden pillar. He stroked the elk's forehead, he lifted the hurt leg and brushed the swollen joint with his hand. The boy called, "Tenyo, help me."

Tenyo studied the elk. The large brown eyes of the elk blinked at him. Tenyo walked around the cave. There were large rocks with which to kill the elk lying everywhere. Tenyo lifted the largest rock he could find. He moved quietly over to the elk, and threw the rock over the elk against the far wall. Tenyo yelled out, "Go, get out of here, go to your mother." The elk cringed at the loud yelling. Tenyo picked up the elk and carried it to the cave opening. "Go to your mother, look, there she is; go, run, run to your freedom." The elk whinnied and ran through the dust to its mother.

Tenyo walked back into the cave. The boy was no longer there. The rope swung back and forth touching the ground. Tenyo studied the ground for footprints, there were none. A rustling sound filled the cave. The four bears came to Tenyo. They sat down leaning against the wooden pillar. Tenyo sat next to them. There they listened to the sounds of the wind. Finally, one bear growled, stood up and beckoned the others to follow. Tenyo joined them. They walked across the flatlands to the cliff path. The sun was now down, the stars shone. Tenyo walked into his cliff dwelling.

His woman was sleeping on her bedroll. He lay down next to her. She turned to him, "Look, look what happened while you were gone." She lifted up a small baby. "He is your son, he has been waiting for you."

Tenyo lay back on his bedroll. His son snuggled against his chest.

Tenyo smiled, he knew this one, he knew the sound of his cry. Tenyo closed his eyes and fell into a peaceful slumber. Brother Moon glowed.

"Grandfather, did you ever have a dream vision?" Grandfather's hands stopped. "What?"

"Grandfather, why is it that men have dream visions and women don't?"

"Women have dream visions. I am not a woman, though, thank God." Grandfather put the basket down. "Yes, I had a dream vision, but it was not as exciting as that of . . . well, a friend of mine. I'll tell you of his."

10

SNAKE BOY

Tsay Pheh (eagle stick) walked along the edge of the high mesa. His grandfather had told him of the spirits that his mother had prayed to when she was young. His mother had been a very gentle woman who liked to help animals, feed birds and sing to the rising sun. Tsay Pheh watched the wild quail waddle along the ground in front of him, searching through the round grass for bugs. Below him was the fast flowing river. From where he stood the river was a small silver thread lying in the turn of the canyon walls. Tsay Pheh let his long hair blow around his shoulders; the winter wind was beginning to blow. His loin cloth would soon be traded for thick leather leggings and his bare chest would be covered with a long hanging leather wrap.

Tsay Pheh walked to the edge of the mesa, his strong fifteen year old arms grabbing the rocks as he swung his thin body down carefully over the tall, pointed lava rocks. His thick soled moccasins barely touched the obstacles that were placed in front of him.

Tsay Pheh watched the silver thread of river getting larger with each descending step. His mother had climbed down these rocks when she was his age, at least that was what his grandfather said. She had come to pray to the spirits of the water. She had been a good, kind woman who had a goodness that was strong enough to make her believe the white men with shiny chests and heads. She had gone with them when they promised to bring food for the old ones. She had agreed to go with them. Her slender body with soft brown eyes was pulled up onto the back of a horse. She rode away with them, the white men with the shiny coverings.

Tsay Pheh jumped down to the green grass of the river valley. The river spoke in hushed tones this day. He squatted down near the cold clear water, "Where are you, Spirits that my mother prayed to? Why didn't you help her?" The river rolled on, saying nothing. Tsay Pheh stood tall and sucked air into his lungs, "*Where are you?*" He called out to the river, the valley and the mesas. His eyes burned, his heart raced with prayers of long ago. Frustration was eating up the spirit in his soul. He turned in disgust and crawled up the rock cliff to the top of the mesa. He turned before running back to his grandfather, "I will be back tomorrow and the day after and the day after until you give me an answer!"

The morning sun came late the next day. Tsay Pheh woke to find his grandfather rubbing pitch into the bottom of a hollowed out cottonwood tree trunk. Grandfather spoke without looking up, "Take this with you today to the river, ride it to the place of the Spirits. Then when you return, you must help with the fields, the old ones, and with your learning rites." Grandfather handed him the hollowed tree, and with the other hand he waved Tsay Pheh off to the mesa. "Go, be gone with you and your dreams, come home a man!"

Tsay Pheh lifted the tree trunk, placing it over one shoulder and hiding part of his head with the other part. His grandfather had been a patient man, perhaps though his wisdom was now going to help Tsay Pheh. Tsay Pheh had a difficult time carrying the boat up the steep mesa to the top. He sat down next to it and watched the sun move steadily over the east plain of the land. The men in shiny skins called this place the land of adventure, his uncle said they called this the New Land, the land that now belonged to the shape of two sticks crossing. This land was of his people and it would always be, no matter who came and called it any name. This land was their soul.

Tsay Pheh lifted up the cottonwood boat; the hard pitch made the boat smell of pine trees. He set the boat down on a group of lava rocks, then carefully carried it down to the bottom of the valley.

The river flowed with the same quietness it had the day before. Birds in great numbers were landing all around the green grass, searching for food. The sky was speckled with white clouds, the clouds over the west mountain were dark and threatening. This was a good sign, for the serpent would come from the sky and bring fertility to the crops and the people. Tsay Pheh put the boat in the water and stepped into its tight shell shape. The river lifted him away from the shore. The boat hit hard against the high rocks that stuck out of the shallow water. The boat gained speed in the deeper water, ramming him against the high sides at each turn. Tsay Pheh felt fear, then dismissed it.

The river moved down through a gorge dropping a long way into a place of darkness. Tsay Pheh tried to reach out and touch the edge of the river in the darkness, but the boat tipped at his every move. Tsay

Pheh felt tired, sleep overtook his body. He dreamed that the boat flowed with the river to a sunny valley.

The sunny valley had deer and elk grazing on the thick rich green grass. Tsay Pheh tried to push his way across the high stones of the river to get out, when he saw a dark man with flowing black hair walking across the river water toward his boat. The man smiled, his strength reaching out to Tsay Pheh. Tsay Pheh watched with wonder as the man was joined by a maiden who was more beautiful than his memory of his mother. She had long flowing hair that touched the water as she walked next to the man. They both waved to him. He lifted his hand. His hand raised up above his shoulder and as it did so, the man and the maiden turned into majestic water serpents. They swam around him, they spoke to him. He could not talk.

The maiden hovered over the boat. She sang a song to the boat, and it rose from the water and lifted high into the air, through the clouds up to the Spirits' land. The boat floated to the high wall of rocks. It settled down slowly onto a spider's web.

Spider Woman emerged from a hole in the rock wall. She slithered over to him, wrapping his boat in her silver threads. She guided a thread around Tsay Pheh, pulling him out of the boat. Tsay Pheh did not move. Spider Woman crawled through a high door, disappearing magically through it. Tsay Pheh stood waiting. The door opened slowly, creaking in the dim light. Two lions jumped through the door rushing at Tsay Pheh. Tsay Pheh jerked back. His leg touched the cottonwood boat. In one movement Tsay Pheh's fingers ripped off a piece of bark. He lifted it high in the air to show strength to the lions; they hesitated, then one jumped at him. Tsay Pheh let the lion knock him down. The lion's strong mouth opened to devour Tsay Pheh, but Tsay Pheh jabbed the cottonwood bark into the lion's mouth. The lion fell dead on top of him. The other lion paced around them watching.

Tsay Pheh gently eased out from under the dead lion. He chanted his prayer of forgiveness to mother earth as he moved opposite the pacing lion. The lion growled, studying Tsay Pheh, but then his attention was diverted to something behind Tsay Pheh. Tsay Pheh whirled around ready to attack. There, sticking out of a hole in a cloud, was the beautiful maiden snake. She beckoned to Tsay Pheh, he backed up to her. She lifted him holding his fragile body in her warm mouth. She released him into the flowing river. He frantically called out to her, she floated away. Tsay Pheh grabbed for her as the water rushed over his head. The handsome male snake bent down placing the cottonwood boat next to Tsay Pheh. Tsay Pheh pulled himself into the boat and once sitting safely he turned to speak his gratitude, when he realized that he was no longer in the river, but the pond near the village.

People ran up to him, cheering and shouting. Tsay Pheh saw his grandfather. Grandfather helped him out of the boat, "You have been gone a long time. See the winter has gone, the crops of spring are waiting to be planted." Tsay Pheh looked at his grandfather's face. His wrinkles were many more than he remembered.

Grandfather studied Tsay Pheh's face, "You have been to the spirits haven't you? You have seen them?" Tsay Pheh nodded to the people. He walked with his grandfather to their home. The mud walls were crumbling, the food was scarce, the rooms still cold. Tsay Pheh thought back to how he had left every day to search for spirits and had left his grandfather alone to do all the work. Tsay Pheh rested for four days. Each night of those four days, Tsay Pheh dreamed of that beautiful snake maiden. He dreamed that she called to him, cried for him, and was still waiting for him.

After irrigating the crops on the fifth morning, Tsay Pheh decided that he would go back over the mesa and look for her. She was there, she was waiting for him. She sang to him. He let her come out of the water to him. They spoke late into the day. Tsay Pheh spent the rest of the following days building a home, a long home with part of it underground. He finished it before the hot warmth of summer came. He went to the river and told the maiden of his plans. He brought with him a mask that his grandfather had made for this purpose. He placed it on her, wrapping her sleek body with a finely woven manta. She moved beside him up the mesa to the new home. He put her mask on a hook near the door, he took her manta and folded it on shelf, he took the beautiful snake maiden and laid her down on the bedroll. He wrapped his warmth around her. She accepted his soul into hers.

Four days later, Tsay Pheh went to the elders and asked for a special feast dance to help his woman through her days of child bearing. They refused. His woman had not been accepted by the people before their union. He would have to find his blessings elsewhere.

Tsay Pheh went to the river, calling out to the spirits there. He was met by the tall man snake. The man snake moved cautiously across the grassy valley to Tsay Pheh. The man snake attacked Tsay Pheh, hitting him with his neck and tail. The man snake had a cross of hard, shiny, sharp material stuck through his tail that slowed his actions, but when it hit Tsay Pheh it cut through the skin. Soon the snake needed to return to the water. Tsay Pheh did not hit or return the brutal feelings to the man snake. The man snake had brought him his boat, had saved him from the fast flowing water. Tsay Pheh respected the man snake's feelings.

Tsay Pheh returned to his home. They lived well throughout the winter, he brought his woman snake fresh water each day. In the spring his woman snake called out in pain. Her screams of pain woke the valley in the night. Her horrible painful groans frightened the people. Tsay Pheh tried desperately to help her. Two little snakes were born. They were not like their mother, they had round stubs on the end of their tails. Tsay Pheh tried to comfort his woman, but her eyes were glazed over, her tongue hung out of her dry mouth.

He feared now for her life and knocked the walls down from his home. He pulled the beautiful snake mother carefully to the river valley. He lay her down near the bank of the river. "Here is your woman, she is returned to you!" The tall man snake appeared and with great care lifted her up and pulled her under the water with him. Tsay Pheh returned to his home. He carried the two baby snakes to the river and tossed them in, watching them play in the water.

Tsay Pheh walked home to his grandfather. Tsay Pheh worked hard with his grandfather. The people left him alone. In the fall several children found two snakes with noise makers on their tails in the village plaza. The snakes spoke and asked for their father. The children laughed at them. One of the snakes bit a child. The child almost died. Tsay Pheh found the snakes, he took them back to the river. The handsome man snake with the cross in his tail agreed to take the snakes to the south.

Tsay Pheh called out to the snake, "Why do you have a cross on your tail?" The tall handsome man snake whispered through the water, "A man with silver on his chest wanted to catch me, all he got was my tail with his silver cross."

Tsay Pheh loped across the high mesa towards home. He had lost his mother to the man with the silver chest and the horse. He had lost a woman that was in the shape of a snake maiden and the two that he had brought into this life. His snake woman he had saved, she was with her people in her place. That was good. Tsay Pheh stayed with his people and taught them the knowledge of his dreams.

Grandfather's voice trembled. He stared at me with sad eyes. I put the willow down and crawled over to him. I held him like a child. Tears ran down the old man's face, falling to his lap. This strong man pushed me away. "It is not right for an old man to show sadness. My life has been good. You are here with me."

81

Grandfather held my hand as we walked back to his home. The sunset was fire red. Grandfather pointed to the horizon. "That is why I live here. Are you warm enough?" I nodded. His eyes were tearing, "This land is ours. It is beautiful, delicate with gentleness. There was much trial in the beginning." Grandfather pulled his wool cap down, his voice softly recounted the times that came before.

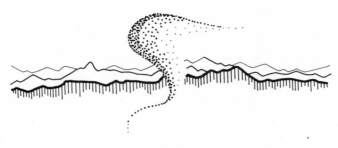

11

AWONAWILONA

The world is pure. The world is empty. No one was here in this place. No one was here to accept Awonawilona. Awonawilona the creature, creator of life, came alone here to this place. He was alone, he made clouds, he dripped moisture on the land, he blew the stillness away.

The light of day was his doing, the warmth of the sun came from his life. Awonawilona made Mother Earth beautiful. Her beauty was so astounding to him that he let her take his moisture to nurture her waters. These waters soon turned to a rich radiant green foam that covered all the brown land. He let the sun dry the waters and some of the brown returned, letting the waterfalls flow freely.

Awonawilona watched the solid brown crust form and he decided that to remember where his favorite places were, he would divide the earth into four directions. Father Sky would watch them, holding them firmly in his arms which covered the full width and breadth of Mother Earth. Awonawilona blew upon her and gave her free life. Awonawilona then left this place to ponder.

Mother Earth rolled around in Father Sky's arms. "What is it that you desire from me?" Father Sky held her tightly to him, "It is time for us to become one, bringing life from us to be here."

Mother Earth let the clouds cover her surface, "It is not time, this place is not prepared for our children, it is not ready. We must work together." She rolled out of his tight grip lying gently in the curve of his strong arm. Father Sky studied the folds of Mother Earth. He did not know what conditions she wanted. He bent his arm lifting her to him, "What is it that you need?"

Mother Earth spoke, "You come down here to this place in the shape of man and I will meet you here as a woman." Father Sky agreed and they met. A brown coiled bowl was in her hand. "There need to be tall shapes such as this over there in that far place to keep the large bodies of water from overflowing onto this place. Large round shapes over in that place to keep the winds from blowing this place flat." She explained her needs to make the right place for her children.

Mother Earth then drank from the brown bowl. Her mouth puckered in bitter response, she spat the liquid back into the bowl. A thick rich foam lay in the bottom of the bowl. She took her thumb and forefinger and squeezed milk from her breast into the bowl. The foam surrounded the milk and grew. Father Sky man smiled, he now knew how creatures were to be nurtured. Mother Earth woman lifted the bowl up into the air, she blew hard into it. The foam was sent upwards into the sky creating thick fat clouds. She blew stronger and a rainbow spread out across the land. Father Sky man knew what was needed. He returned to his original shape and, rising above the clouds and the rainbow, he let a light rain fall from his being. Mother Earth changed into her original shape, for deep inside of her life had started.

Life was growing in the deepest sanctum of her, in the bottom of her four wombs.

Father Sky glowed with his joy. He opened his hands to show his thanks. In every crease from fingertip to palm lay multi-colored sparkling seeds of corn. Very carefully he lifted his gift up above Mother Earth, placing the brilliant stars as a remembrance that life is fragile, it is to be respected.

Awonawilona took the stars to be divided into the four directions, north, south, east, west, and to move constantly upward and downward. Awonawilona turned from that duty to bless the breasts of Mother Earth. His chanting song gave her golden grains of corn which would nurture the people that were to come. Father Sky worked hard shaping the earth to the needs of those who would live upon her. Deep down in the bowels of generation, life began to take form. Beings were born. They were confused, groping in the darkness. They cried out in horrible sounds, slithering and struggling. They did not understand their purpose. In time they learned to share and work together to gain their needs. Conversation was a strange grunting.

Poahaiyangk-yo was a being among them. He was a creature who had learned to watch, listen and understand. There was a small shading of light which at certain times was more noticeable. Poahaiyangk-yo studied this light for four days. He found that when he was near it, there was warmth. In the quiet time Poahaiyangk-yo made his escape to the warmer place.

He was guided along a thin fragile path to the third womb where no one else had ever been. He followed the light, kneeling in a billowy foamy swamp to listen. There he raised his head and chanted to the spirits to release those still submerged in the fourth womb.

Sun heard the chanting and gave strength to Poahaiyangk-yo. As he did so, the fertility of Father Sky fell into the billowy swamp and life grew. Twins were born, they were named the Preceder and the Follower. Father Sky gave the colors of the rainbow and the thick heavy clouds (which bring confusion) to the twins. They were to use these as tools for their purpose.

They flew on the thick clouds to Poahaiyangk-yo. The clouds echoed through tunnels as they called out to him. Poahaiyangk-yo cowered in the darkness listening to voices call out around him. The Preceder dropped from the thick clouds to stand in front of Poahaiyangk-yo. Follower followed behind. They asked what was needed from them. Poahaiyangk-yo told them of the people in the lower womb. The twins flew down to the place where the others were. They moved among them quietly talking with them, holding them, comforting each creature. When they were ready, the Preceder and the Follower found thick vines and bound them together to make a rope and they helped guide the creatures one over the other, hand by hand, foot by foot up over into the next womb. Each hand that touched the rope of vines brought forth a burst of life in the rope. Branches grew in abundance, letting more and more of the creatures move upward. Poahaiyangk-yo stood at the top of the rope greeting his fellow creatures to the new place.

The third womb had more space, but when all the creatures of different shapes and sizes kept coming up from below, there was a tightness that brought arguing. The twins spoke with Poahaiyangk-yo and decided that the time had come to move again. Poahaiyangk-yo decided that this time he would not be the leader, he would help with those who were less able to climb.

The twins could not find any vines in this womb. They lifted up the creatures onto each others' backs, thus making a living ladder. The voices echoed through the tunnel. Crying, screaming, and orders mixed together. Many fell down unable to keep hold, falling all the way down to darkness. Some returned, but they were not the same. They acted different, they were cold and disfigured.

The second womb was filled with a soft light. There was open land with soft waters flowing. The creatures learned enjoyment, and their own communication. The boundaries between groups of creatures narrowed, fighting broke out between the stronger groups. This was not good.

The twins divided the animals and men into six groups. There was a great deal of pushing and shoving as they climbed once more into the world of Mother Earth.

The bright light on the level of birth was that of a dark night with thunder clouds. The people and animals discovered what union means and the pleasure of giving birth. The Preceder and Follower taught the people how to make shelter and to find food. Father Sky kept the sky dark. The twins approached Father Sky on their thick clouds and asked him to lighten the sky more and more each day.

Father Sky let the stars shine, showing the creatures his gift to them. They were frightened. They ran about screaming, digging frantically with webbed fingers and feet to make hollows in which to hide. Their long tails kept them from moving very fast, their thick eyelids blinked anxiously trying to remove the hurt. Scales fell from their tough skins, owl shaped eyes peered at their neighbors while large droopy ears kept them from hearing clearly.

Father Sky let the star Sirius shine down for four nights without day. The creatures slowly accepted the light. On the fourth day, Father Sky let the sun shine through thick white clouds. The creatures were terrified, the brightness shone through their thin eyelids scorching their eyes.

It is said that Awonawilona came down at this time and carefully placed blue spruce sap on the thin eyelids, toughening them so that when they were closed the light could not enter through them. Awonawilona then trimmed the webs away from between the fingers and toes giving an extra bend in the fingers for grasping and holding objects. Awonawilona then pulled the legs longer, cutting off the tail at the back bone. He taught the people how to wrap their bodies and place wrapped willow on their feet to protect them from the rocks. This was good.

There were other creatures which Awonawilona did not change. They were beings more gruesome than you can imagine. The area between the mountains was desolate and empty. At night the ground rumbled and shook. The people were fearful that the earth would swallow them without warning.

Awonawilona spoke to the twins and told them to take those who could travel back to the Shipap, or the place of emergence. The sky turned dark. Lightning snakes fell from the sky burning forests and trees. The Preceder called Spider Woman to make a web strong enough to keep the creatures together. Follower took the strong web and tied it to each person. They were led back to the Shipap and arrived there as the sun was rising. There they found a stillness of the earth that let them grow the seeds that were given to them. Life was balanced.

Awonawilona told the people that this place was Mother Earth, their mother. He explained that animals and people were not complete in their growth but in time they would be. They should be wary of monsters, volcanos (which were mountains that had not finished forming) and giants whose purpose was not yet known. It was taught that the northern most point in the sky was where the Lion lived, the western point was the home of the Wolf, the southern mountains kept the Wise Bear and the eastern wooded area and flat lands held the Mighty Badger. The Dew People would guard the crops and water them every morning and evening as long as the people were respectful of each other and Mother Earth.

Grandfather patted my shoulder, "Let's go in now. The sun is over the edge." I followed him. The fire crackled in the fireplace.

"Where is Awonawilona now?" I asked pulling off my heavy boots. "He is there." Grandfather pointed up, "This story is not of the northern Pueblos, it is from the south. It is worth remembering."

Grandfather took a hot shower while I did some laundry in his old washing machine. The dryer was the clothes line in the back room.

I took out the hamburger meat and started to brown it in the big cast iron frying pan. Grandfather always fixed the chili in the meat so I set it aside for him. I sliced some potatoes and fried them nice and brown. Grandfather loved brussel sprouts steamed over a pot of boiling water with lemon and butter. Grandfather came up behind me and studied the pots on the stove. "Very good. Careful with those sprouts, don't burn them."

Grandfather reached up to the chili ristra and pulled off a dried red chili. He crumpled it in his hand over a bowl. Then he took a round ball and smashed the pieces of chili into small particles. This he put in the browned hamburger. He reached over my head to the spice rack shaking spices into the mixture. "Do you like a lot of salt in your chili?" He held the salt shaker in mid-air.

"No, not really, it hides the wonderful flavor of all those other spices."

He nodded approval and tipped the salt shaker. "It is important to eat salt. I'll tell you why."

12

SALT WOMAN

At a certain Pueblo there came a visitor, an old woman who was called Salt Woman. She came with her son who was old enough to work, farm or at least do something productive, but he wouldn't — all he did was follow his mother around. Salt Woman begged in every Pueblo that she visited for that was their only way of getting food. Now it is important to know that Salt Woman was not very patient. How she came to have a son, I will never know. Salt Woman wore her long white, shiny hair down, down to her ankles it hung. She wore ragged clothes that were clean and white, she had no shoes and the soles of her feet were thick with old callouses. Her son was small for his age, he rarely looked up at anyone, but humbled himself even to the barking dogs that growled at him.

The Salt Woman went graciously from door to door in this Pueblo and at each door she was turned away. The people did not know of her or why anyone would let an old woman with such beauty and grace walk about begging. They were embarrassed to have her at their door. These were good people but they were worried about the social connotations that would come from having her in their homes. They were all preparing for a sacred feast dance. All the food they had was being cooked, the people were fasting in preparation for the feast that was to start the next day and last for four days.

Salt Woman held her head high, she did not stop but continued calling out at each door, pushing her son forward, telling the people that her son was starving and they were in need of food. The people hid from her or scolded her. Salt Woman walked through the whole Pueblo, no one had given them food. Her eyes were filled with bitterness.

She pulled her son to her as they left this one Pueblo. Salt Woman chose a path that went through a dense forest. There were children playing among the trees. Salt Woman reached into her bundle and pulled out a large salt crystal. It glittered in what light there was. The children ran up to her pushing and shoving, each one wanted to see or hold that beautiful crystal. The Salt Woman's eyes glowed, "Certainly you can see it. Those who can hang from the highest tree limb may be able to hold the crystal." Her son started to climb with the other children. She held him back. The children were climbing as fast as they could. They were now way up above her head.

"Now swing way out on the tree branches." The children did as she asked.

"Your parents would not feed us, they were too selfish to be kind to an old woman and her young son, therefore I turn you all into chapparel jays. Fly off, fly away." The children were screaming one moment and the next the screeching of birds could be heard back to the Pueblo.

The Salt Woman pulled her son to her side giving him a firm pat. "Let us go." They walked until they came to another Pueblo. There the people greeted Salt Woman and invited her into their homes and fed her and her son very well. Salt Woman was pleased. She let her son play with the children while she spoke to the people. "You have been kind to us and for this I would like to repay you. Here, you may have some of my skin." She scraped off some powdery skin. The people were unsure of it. Salt Woman invited the women into the cooking room and explained to them the proper cooking methods for using salt. She showed them how to dry meat with salt, to flavor breads with salt, and how to use salt in medicine.

"Here, you add it to your food. It will taste better and it will keep you healthy."

The women brought the foods that she had helped them prepare. It was bitter, but good. Salt Woman told them that if they ever needed more of this that they could come to the Lake of Salt, she would gladly give them more. "You must come with respect, for my magic is very strong."

Grandfather placed the food on the table. We were both very hungry. "Where is the Lake of Salt?" Grandfather mumbled through his mouthful, "South of Santa Fe."

Grandfather helped with the dishes. The water cooled fast in the wash basin. The old china stood proudly on the wooden hutch. The woodstove hummed and whistled. We had discussed my mother and father throughout the evening meal. Grandfather felt that I should not continue at the university until I had found a man.

I was wise enough to keep silent and listen. "You will end up lonely, an old hag. You don't want that, do you?" I handed him the last coffee cup. Grandfather pulled out what remained of his cigar and stuck it between his crooked teeth. "I will tell you a story. This one is from the southern Pueblo."

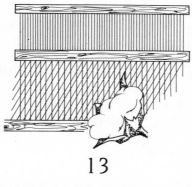

13

WOMAN WEAVER

There is a beautiful village to the east of us. The village used to be a Pueblo but it was taken over by the Spanish at one time. In this village lived a man and a woman. They had tried for many years to have a child. When they had given their spirit the freedom to choose for them, they had a very beautiful daughter, who was also very stubborn. She grew very fast, as only children can and when she was old enough to choose a man, she announced that she had no interest in men. She had her work to do; after all now that she could weave, she could put all her energy into helping the people she loved most, her mother and father. If she could help them and make their lives easier what more could she ask for? She picked wild cotton from the fields, she combed the cotton, spun it and wove it into beautiful leggings for the dancers. She traded and sold the leggings for food and supplies. This she did until all the people had bought or traded for her leggings.

Next she decided that she would weave mantas. She worked very hard picking the cotton, washing, combing it. She threaded a loom that she had made and wove a fine, soft, solid white manta. She draped it across the loom carefully, gathered up the finer cotton threads and dyed them with natural dyes that she had collected. She worked hard and long on this manta. People would come and watch her work, and were amazed. Soon the first manta was finished. Its beauty was astounding. She gave it to her parents to take into the village to trade. The daughter was very tired and she slept while her parents were gone.

They woke her when they returned. They had traded the manta for many fine things and they had a long list of others who wanted her to weave them a manta as fine with the deep rich colors. The beautfiul, but stubborn girl went to work and made many more mantas. The men were proud of this woman who could make such beauty. They wanted to court her and win her as their woman. They gathered together and decided to have a special dance for her. They sent runners to ask her to come to the dance. She sent them away saying, "I am busy, I have to work. I do not have time for play." The runners told the people, the people put on their dancing costumes and went to her home. They danced for her, but she took no notice, she was too busy working.

Her mother and father were very worried about her, they wanted her to have a family and rest as well as work. The day after the dance, men came to her door and brought her gifts, some cotton, some little stone birds, and some brought fetishes. She ignored them. She shook her head saying, "I am happy here, I work, I have whatever I need here in front of me. I do not need a man." The men left her alone after that.

One young man, who had found the woman to be a challenge, listened to her words and felt a great sadness. He talked with his father about the problems of women. The father told his son a long story and in the morning the young man decided that he would win the favor of this young woman.

He went up into the mountains and gathered up wild plum branches. He searched for the most purple plums and those that were red orange and full of juice. Strong long branches were laid side by side and wrapped with a strong leather thong. He returned to his home placing the wild plums in a pouch. The man put on his white moccasins, his white leggings, and his white loin cloth. He then gathered up the pouch of wild plums, the big bulk of plum branches and went to the plaza by the daughter's home.

There he called out to his friends and started to dance and chant. The woman looked up to see who was dancing. The man reached into his bag and showed the wild plums to the people around him, then he ate some.

The daughter rushed outside. "Please let me have some wild plums?" He kept eating them, he gave her none. He rubbed his palms together saying, "If you would like some then you must come with me and pick them." She hurriedly said "Yes." In her eagerness she dropped her cotton and the brushes she was using to comb the cotton on the ground. She loved the taste of wild plums and she could use the branch to dye cloth.

He led her up a hill, down a long path, to a beautiful forest area. There were the wild plums. He picked them for her, he fed them to her, he stroked her hair, he let her rest, and he gave her warmth. She enjoyed it.

When she returned home, her parents met them at the door. Her father pulled the young man aside. The mother cried and tore her hair. "Why do you do this after we believed you? You who would not even consider a man, you run off with someone your family has not ever met?"

The father put the young man through a testing. When he saw how well the young man did, he knew that his daughter had chosen well. The beautiful, but stubborn daughter had many children with her man and she still works very hard making clothes for the people and her family. She has also learned to listen to her elders and respect their wisdom.

Grandfather cleared his throat, "What do you think of that?" He lit a kitchen match lifting it to the cigar stub. I watched from my cozy spot on the couch near the fireplace. The coals were glowing orange. I was brave enough to answer him, "It was all right, but do you remember this story?"

It was now my time to tell a story to the storyteller. Grandfather puffed on his cigar knowing that I had to pick each word carefully.

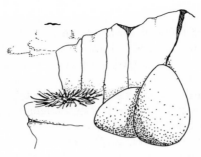

14

MOON WOMAN

Long before the outsiders came to New Mexico, this world was peaceful and managed very well by those who lived here. In those days, Nah-chu-ru-chu, "The Bluish Light Of Dawn," dwelt in a special village, he was a leader of his people. A weaver by trade, his long loom hung from the vigas of his room. He wove the strong black mantas or robes.

Nah-chu-ru-chu was young, wise in medicine, and tall, strong and handsome. He did not want a woman. Women would bring him gifts to get his attention, but he showed no interest in them, only in his work. Two women who admired him were sisters, the Yellow Corn Sisters, who held great magic powers. Some said that they were witches, others said that their powers were great in good and evil. I'm not going to say one way or the other.

One day the sisters came to Nah-chu-ru-chu's house to win his favor. They talked to him about the reasons he should choose a woman. They talked to him all morning, expecting him to offer them a mid-day meal.

He sat and listened to them going on and on and thought of the weaving he was missing. The Yellow Corn Sisters did not stop, they continued to tell him how dirty his house was, how unkept his clothes were, on and on they talked until the time of the setting sun. Finally they took their gifts and left him alone.

Nah-chu-ru-chu decided that to prevent this from happening again he would choose a woman. He visited his friend who had a deep rolling voice. They talked about women for some time. The friend told him he should marry a strong plump wife who could bear many children and cook good food.

It was decided the friend would walk through the Pueblo and announce that at the end of four days Nah-chu-ru-chu would choose who he wanted for a woman. When his friend returned he suggested to

Nah-chu-ru-chu that he best think the idea over, for he could very easily pick a woman that interrupted his work. Nah-chu-ru-chu groaned, "What do I do now?" His friend smiled, "Have a testing." Nah-chu-ru-chu was getting discouraged as he and his friend walked back to his house. There on the side of the wall he had a well-sanded, well-worn, shiny water gourd that hung over the water bucket. The two friends spoke of the gourd and agreed to the test.

On the fourth day women could come and throw cornmeal at the gourd. If the corn was ground fine enough it would stick to the gourd. The woman who could get her cornmeal to stick to the shiny gourd would become his woman.

The women gathered the finest corn they could find in their gardens, they ground and ground their cornmeal chanting magic spells, praying to the Spirits for theirs to be the finest cornmeal.

Now, off in the hills not far from the Pueblo, lived Moon Woman. She had not decided yet if she wanted to go up into the sky to live or stay down with the people. She was very beautiful, although she was blind in one eye which glowed a deep gold in the night. On this particular day, she decided to go into the Pueblo and visit some friends. On her way through the Pueblo she met the Yellow Corn Sisters. They were dressed in their finest clothes each carrying a pouch close to her bosom. She greeted them with a friendly remark. They laughed at her. "You cannot grind cornmeal, so you cannot be Nah-chu-ru-chu's woman. You have no corn and you have neither a matate or a mano to grind it with, hah, hah!" They hurried away from her.

Moon Woman had watched Nah-chu-ru-chu many times, he was a very attractive man. Moon Woman decided to go and watch anyway. As she walked through the Pueblo, she noticed the long line of women gathering outside Nah-chu-ru-chu's home, each with a pouch of cornmeal in their hands. They talked among themselves saying, "We have the finest cornmeal, it will stick!" They waited patiently for the testing to begin.

The threw their handfuls of cornmeal, but it did not stick at all. The Yellow Corn Sisters were very angry and instead of moving on as the other women had done, they stood there and kept throwing and throwing at the gourd. Last of all Moon Woman came with a handful of cornmeal that she had found on the ground and tossed it at the gourd. The Yellow Corn Sisters jeered at her saying, "You cannot get that cornmeal to stick, you are a fine joke." But Moon Woman carefully threw her cornmeal at the gourd, it stuck. It was ground so fine and had been walked on so much that it was a fine powder. Every tiny bit of it stuck to the gourd.

When Nah-chu-ru-chu saw that, he went to the Moon Woman saying, "You are the one who will be my woman. You shall never want for anything since I have so much." He gave her beautiful clothes and she accepted these things gracefully. But the Yellow Corn Sisters who had seen all this went away filled with anger and ideas.

Nah-chu-ru-chu and his Moon Woman were very happy together. She could cook a great meal for one or for many, she could clean with a wink from her orange eye. Her man Nah-chu-ru-chu brought her home large deer and rabbits. He spoke to her often about keeping away from the Yellow Corn Sisters. She promised to stay away from them.

One day the Yellow Corn Sisters came to the house and said, "Friend Nah-chur-ru-chu, we are going to the plains to gather amole soap, will you not let your wife go with us?"

"Oh, yes, she may go." Then he spoke to her alone, "Make sure that whatever they suggest, you refuse!"

Moon Woman promised and left with the Yellow Corn Sisters. They picked amole soap for some time, then they came to a drying spring. "Oh, let's stop and get some water to drink." The Yellow Corn Sisters offered her some water. The Moon Woman said she was not thirsty, remembering what her husband had told her. The sisters then looked at themselves in the water. "Oh, look how silly we are staring at ourselves. Come here Moon Woman and look at yourself, see how silly the water makes us look?" The Moon Woman was eager to have fun and see what was so funny and went to the spring's edge to look.

The Yellow Corn Sisters threw her into the spring and drowned her. They carried dirt and buried Moon Woman in the drying spring, packing the dirt down as they did so. They laughed at their cleverness and went home.

Later that evening, Nah-chu-ru-chu met them. "Where is my woman?"

They smiled at him, "Oh, isn't she home yet?" They danced away from him.

"Oh no," Nah-chur-ru-chu thought, "They have done something to her." He went away searching for his woman. After four days, he gave up and went to the top of the ladder of the kiva. He sat there and held his head in great dispair. He sat for days, never speaking, never eating, never moving. The children looked up at the motionless figure. The old men shook their heads and said, "We are in for evil times."

Later the people gathered together and agreed that they should help him find his woman. They each took some of the sacred smoking weed wrapped in a corn husk and went to the eagle who has the sharpest eyes of all. They asked him to look for Moon Woman. The eagle took the offering and smoked the smoke prayer, then he went winging upward into the sky. Higher and higher he rose while his keen eyes noted every stick, stone and animal. But with his sharp eyes he could not find the woman. He told them, "I went up to see the whole world but I could not find her."

Then the people went to coyote whose nose is the best in the whole world. The coyote smoked the smoke prayer and started off sniffing the ground. He trotted all over the earth, but at last he too came back without finding what he sought. Then they asked the badger to search, for he is good at digging. The badger tunneled all over but could not find the woman.

The people had not enough water to keep them alive. They went at last to P'ah-ku-ee-teh-ay and asked him to find the dead Moon Woman. He soared higher than the clouds and searched with his great might, but he returned sadly saying, "Nothing, I found nothing." He turned to leave, then stopped, "I did see a flower, a beautiful white delicate flower sticking up from a little mound."

Nah-chu-ru-chu's eyes looked up at the bird, "Oh, friend take us to that white flower." In a few minutes the buzzard of death brought them to the white flower. Nah-chu-ru-chu held up the flower crying, "Shu-nah, seeking her, seeking her." He sang this as he moved to the dirt mound. The dirt lifted up and there under the dirt was a manta. He kept singing and the dirt lifted. Then there were two layers of manta. Soon, a figure sat up, it was his Moon Woman. She was alive and more beautiful than ever.

For four days the people danced and sang in the plaza. Nah-chu-ru-chu was happy again, and the rain began to fall. The dry earth drank and was lush and all the dead plants came back to life. When his Moon Woman told him what the Yellow Corn Sisters had done, he was very angry. He made a hoop to play the hoop game with, and he painted it and put many strings across it and decorated it with beaded buckskin. "Now," he said, "You ask the Yellow Corn Sisters to go out and play with you." Moon Woman was astonished, "You want me to invite them out to play a game?" Nah-chu-ru-chu nodded. It was not her place to question him.

That day Moon Woman invited the Yellow Corn Sisters to go out and play the hoop game. They went up to the edge of the llano and there she let them get a glimpse of the beautiful hoop. "Oh, give us that, Moon Woman." They started to tug at her arm. She pushed them away saying, "Well, if you really like it we can play the hoop game. I will stand here and you there, and if when I throw it to you, you catch it, you may have it."

The Yellow Corn Sisters stood a little way down the hill and she threw the beautiful hoop up in the air. It glistened, falling and rolling and they both grasped it at the same time. Then, instead of the Yellow Corn Sisters, there were two snakes with ugly bodies and horrid faces. "There, now your home will be in the rocks and cliffs forever, but you must never, never be found in the Pueblo, and you must never bite a person. Remember you are still women and you must be humble." Then the Moon Woman went to her man. They were very happy. The sister snakes live in the rocks and they never come into the Pueblo.

Grandfather snorted. I turned to look at him. He was sound asleep in his big red easy chair. I pulled the cigar from his mouth, placing it in the ashtray. "Good night, Mother Earth."

The dogs woke me in the morning. Grandfather was outside feeding them. Each dog's howl was in a different tone, together they filled the air with a blood-curdling sound. I hurried to get dressed, rushing into the kitchen to start the wood stove. It was already going with hot coffee bubbling in a deep pan. Dry dog food crunchies were all over the floor. Grandfather kicked some across the room as he entered. "Well, it's about time." He shook his head at me.

The coffee was poured into deep mugs and set on the table. I finished sweeping up the dog food and sat down to join him. "You look well baked this morning." He slurped on his coffee. "You know what I mean by that?" Somehow my head wasn't ready for a confrontation this morning. I tried to ignore his bad mood.

"Do you know what I mean by that?" He asked again. I shook my head. Grandfather leaned back in his chair and told me.

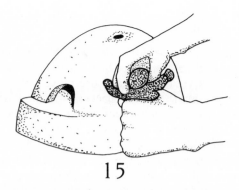

15

WELL BAKED GOODS

The spirit maker made the world but he felt that it was not quite right, not yet. Something was missing. He watched his animals move about on the land. He decided to put some people down to walk around with the animals. The spirit maker came down to earth and made himself a horno. He gathered up some clay and made it into an image like himself. The spirit maker put the clay image into the horno. Then he realized that there was no wood in the horno, so he went off for firewood. Well, old coyote who was hunting around saw the horno. He peeked inside and saw the small image placed inside. He took it out and reshaped it, then when he got bored he put it back inside the horno.

The spirit maker returned and placed the wood inside the horno. He waited until the fire had cooled before he pulled out the image. By now Coyote had returned to see what was going on in the horno. The spirit maker pulled out the figure. It walked upon all four legs, it barked and wagged its tail. "Oh, no," said spirit maker, "This looks like coyote." Coyote came over and asked, "What is wrong with that?" Spirit maker knew better than to argue with Coyote. Spirit maker continued to make another image. He watched the four legged creature that coyote made. He shook his head, it was not a very good likeness of Coyote, it was a dog.

Coyote came over and watched him. Spirit maker said, "Don't bother me anymore, go away."

Spirit maker made two this time. They would be companions this way, someone to be with in life. The clay was drying and difficult to shape. "What's wrong here, this one has something different and this one is cracking. Well I'd better cook them or they will not come out right at all." Spirit maker did so and he made man and woman. He placed them in the horno, then walked around watching coyote play with the dog.

Coyote said, "They are done, they are burning up!" Spirit maker pulled them out of the hot fire. They were all white and pale. "Oh, Coyote they are not yet done. I can't use these." He tossed them over the horno. Then he made another pair just the same as the others that were underdone. He waited longer this time, he was ready to pull them out when coyote yelled at him, "Not yet, not yet." So they waited longer.

Finally the spirit maker pulled them out and they were black as night. "I cannot use these either, you give me bad advice, I do not know why I listen to you." Spirit maker threw these farther right across the waters of the ocean. Then he started again. This time he did not listen to the coyote. He pulled the figures out when he felt the time was right. They were just what he wanted, they looked like him. They walked, laughed, sang, and moved about like he did. He was very pleased. He called coyote to him saying, "These are just right!"

Grandfather laughed loudly. The sky was overcast, the wind was blowing hard. Today would be a weaving day, perhaps a good day.

Grandfather pulled out the wet willow withes and set them before me. "Here, you strip the bark off these. Those in that bucket are a nice color, we'll leave them the way they are." Grandfather sat cross legged on his old rug. The widow could be heard calling her cat. Her voice carried even in the high wind. Grandfather shook his head. "Do you know the story of the White Buffalo?" I nodded, it was one of his favorites. Usually he told this story to a strange woman that was showing off to the men. Grandfather did not look at me, he went on with his weaving and his story.

16

GREAT WHITE BUFFALO

The people were moving from place to place. They stopped at a large lake to gather water. There had been much confusion on the journey as to who was the rightful chief. The Elders decided to stop here by this lake and they would hold a meeting. This meeting would determine if the chief who was now head of the council would remain, or be replaced by the oldest man of the Badger Clan. The women were given duties that needed to be finished by the time of the setting sun. Each woman was given a specific duty. This duty was also a reflection of her man and his ability to be in the clan. The women held great strength, but it was strength not readily noticeable. Their strength was in the teaching and guarding of the children. Uncles were to teach the chants and dances to the boys, but the women taught the children respect, honor, humility and most of all, harmony with the earth itself.

The chief's wife, who had not yet come with child, was told to go out into the lake and bring fresh clear water to the Elders. This was an honor to her and to her man. Her man was a powerful man in the ways of wisdom and in his possession was a great white buffalo head. To show his honor for his woman he took the great white buffalo head and placed it on the bank of the lake. He smiled at the beauty of his wife. She would stand proudly on that buffalo head and lift up the water, the water of purity for the Elders.

The chief's woman with the flowing manta of soft deer hide stopped before putting her foot down on the great white buffalo head. "What a pity that you are dead, you are such a beautiful buffalo." When she stopped speaking the buffalo head lifted up and became a full white buffalo. He lifted her onto his massive back and galloped off with her. She dropped her basket and held on tightly to his long flowing mane.

The other women were too busy with their own problems to notice what happened. Everyone was hurrying to finish the cooking, the bedding for the children and the men were busy with their meeting. The sun was going down and the chief was worried about his woman. He went to the lake to get her. All he found was her basket and the hoof prints of the buffalo.

He ran back to his people telling them that his woman had disappeared with the large buffalo head. The people were frightened for the white buffalo had great powers and the chief's woman was indeed beautiful and the buffalo would want to keep her. The people were very frightened for this was very great magic.

The chief stormed away from his people with anger. He grabbed his pouch, walking off across the foothills to the plains. By morning the man was tired and his steps were faltering, he almost stepped on mother spider who was tending her young. Mother spider called up to him asking him of his destination. He was thankful to sit and talk with someone. Mother spider gave some cornmeal to him telling him to take it to mother fox who would help him. The chief lifted his weary body off the ground to continue his search. He went to mother fox who was very pleased to get the cornmeal. She listened to the chief's problem and told him that who he really needed to see was someone who could quietly get underground and take his woman away from the buffalo without being seen. For if the buffalo caught him it would be terrible. White buffalo had great power that could hurt not only the chief and his wife but the Indian people as well. The chief was willing to risk danger for he cared very deeply for his woman.

That night the mother fox led the chief to mother gopher. Mother gopher was not too pleased about helping a stranger in the middle of the night. Mother fox gave some cornmeal to mother gopher and after a small conference, mother gopher agreed to help. Mother fox stayed and looked after the little gophers. The mother gopher tunneled up into the middle of the white buffalo's bed. The chief's woman was pressed between the white buffalo and his oldest son. She had on a dress that was covered with bells. Mother gopher whispered to her, "Roll the dress up around your knees." The chief's woman whispered that she had a headdress of feathers that would rustle if she moved. Mother gopher told her, "Don't move your head." Mother gopher led the chief's woman down through the tunnel.

The chief was glad to see his woman, they started to talk. Mother gopher told them to hurry back to their people. They ran to the mountains, it was night and they slept. In the morning the chief swept the ground with spruce boughs to clear the scent so that the buffalo could not smell them. The chief's woman gathered up the blanket. The buffalo came and smelled where they were. The chief and his woman hid in a tree. The other buffalo bellowed to the great white buffalo. He rubbed noses with the other buffalo.

The great white buffalo lifted his great furry head and with his brown eyes he saw them hiding in the tree. He turned to lope a distance, then charged the tree. A magpie landed near the chief and told him that if he shot an arrow into the base of buffalo's tail, he would kill the buffalo. The chief pulled a long arrow, loaded it onto his bow and shot, killing the white buffalo. The other buffalo ran off frightened.

The chief and his woman climbed down the tree. The chief dragged the great white buffalo into the foothills. He lay the buffalo out and cut it up. He told his woman to gather dried wood, they would have a feast tonight. The woman pulled down her beautiful dress, she patted it, it was of soft hide. From her arms hung the cat claws that the white buffalo had given her. The woman did not move. She stood aside as her man gathered the wood, built the fire, and skewered the meat, roasting it over the hot fire.

She could not watch the fire where the meat of the white buffalo was cooking. The chief tried to take off her crown of feathers and burn it. The woman pulled away from him as tears ran down her face. The chief ordered her to take it off, "I have saved you and your people, now show me that you care for me, or are you still in love with the white buffalo while he is cooking there?" The chief, in his anger, pulled an arrow and shot his woman.

When the chief returned to his people with the white buffalo meat he told them of his woman. His eyes were filled with sadness, he said, "From now on, any woman who is not loyal to her man shall have done to her what I have done to my woman."

The basket was almost finished. Fingers molded colors into works of art. Grandfather's voice didn't stop. He grabbed more willow from my pile. "Testing is not only for those who are loyal to those they love, but also for those who want to better their lives." Water dripped to the rhythm of Grandfather's voice.

17

CLOUD EATER

There was a time when the monsters still roamed freely on the earth. Father Sky had no way of controlling them or keeping them away from his creatures. Mother Earth nurtured all things with her care. This allowed a monster named Cloud Eater to make his home in the East on a mountain top. Larger than the highest mountain, Cloud Eater's mouth could reach all the way to the West. His appetite was gluttonous and his basic food was clouds. Sometimes he was greedier than other times, and when this was so, the entire land received no rain. Also, if there were no clouds, he had a tendency to eat other things; for instance, small animals, large animals, people or birds. His taste buds were not terribly fussy. But when he ate clouds, all the clouds in the sky, all the clouds that happened to be just starting out in the crystal blue of the above, well then the fields withered and died and all of the animals starved. Only the people who had stored food could survive and they too, had to be cautious of the Cloud Eater.

Many men had hunted for Cloud Eater but none had survived. Far toward the west, Ahaiyuta lived with his old grandmother on the heights of Maize Mountain. Strong as his father, the Sun, and as fast as an antelope, Ahaiyuta waited for his chance to prove that he was now a man.

One day he went to his grandmother with a request. "Grandmother, what can I do to become a man?"

"There is a great task to be done which has never been accomplished." Grandmother spoke softly. Grandmother was a small woman, but it was known that her powers were great. Grandmother had taken on the task of raising her grandson after her own son had died from starvation. Her son's woman was still alive, but now she lived with another man who was also very sick and poorly.

104

"I am not afraid," Ahaiyuta replied, "Tell me how I can be respected as a man." Grandmother's eyes sparkled. Her grandson was a strong boy. He had been well fed and well taught.

"You must kill Cloud Eater so that the rain will fall again bringing life back to this earth." Grandmother lowered her eyes to hide her hope.

"Who is Cloud Eater?"

Grandmother told him how Cloud Eater had killed many people with his greedy appetite, for as long as she could remember.

"Let me kill Cloud Eater, my grandmother." And the boy lifted up his strongest bow and his longest arrows.

"First you must find Cloud Eater, my grandson." She went to a basket and removed four feathers.

"You must put the red feather in your hair, it will take you to Cloud Eater. This blue feather has powerful medicine that will enable you to talk to the animals and to understand them. With the yellow feather in your possession, you can make yourself as small as any animal and just as able."

"But what is the black feather for?" asked the boy.

"That is the most powerful of all of the four feathers, you must guard them carefully and never lose or misplace them." Grandmother sat down holding the black feather. "The black feather, Grandson, will give you the stength of a herd of deer or that of a mountain lion as he runs. Only use this arrow when you are ready or you will lose its powers."

Ahaiyuta stuck the red feather in his hair and strode off toward the East. The land was hot and barren as he traveled, following the direction of the red feather. The air became hot, the desert growth was sparse. The ground became more parched and there were large cracks in the ground. For several hours he had seen no animals. He began to stumble and fall when a sound shrieked out in the silence. A mole stared up at him, chattering violently. Ahaiyuta knelt down, putting the blue feather in his hair. The mole said, "If you would get your foot off my paw, it would be a great sign of manhood." Ahaiyuta lifted his foot, the mole gave a sigh of relief. "What are you doing out here? Don't you know that Cloud Eater will eat you up if he finds you?"

"Can you tell me where Cloud Eater lives?" Ahaiyuta asked.

"Cloud Eater's home is just a few days' journey to the east, but you must be careful for if he sees you, you will be dead," said Mole. "I would be dead by now if my home were not underground where it is safe."

"Can I go through your tunnels to Cloud Eater's Pueblo?" The mole shook his head, "You are too big for my small tunnels or I would gladly help you." Ahaiyuta placed the yellow feather in his hair. Instantly Ahaiyuta became as small as Mole and he stepped into the underground tunnel.

"My," sighed Mole. "You have powers, you are as brave as I am. Follow me."

He followed Mole. Ahaiyuta noticed the pockets of food and water that Mole had. They stopped for food everytime the tunnel moved upward, careful not to leave any waste.

On the fourth day, Mole stopped. "We will soon be under Cloud Eater." The ground began to shake and there was a thundering sound. The tunnel shook and some stones loosened.

"Cloud Eater is above us," Mole said to Ahaiyuta, "He is sleeping; the noise you hear is his snoring. We must be very quiet."

"I hear Cloud Eater's heart beating," Ahaiyuta stuck the fourth feather, the black one, in his hair. "Now I can kill him," he said as he felt his body tingling.

Pulling his bow, Ahaiyuta stood strong. Ahaiyuta aimed at the place in the tunnel above where the sound of the Cloud Eater's heart was pounding. When he released his arrow the world around him went completely dark. The ground caved in and Ahaiyuta and Mole were buried in a mass of dirt and rocks. The ground was still shaking when Mole dug Ahaiyuta out of the debris.

"You killed Cloud Eater," Mole danced for joy. "The earth buried you and Cloud Eater is dead, but I dug you out. See your arrow sticking out of Cloud Eater's heart?"

The two walked out of the tunnels to look up into the sky which was growing dark. Soon the rain came, bringing life back to the barren earth. Ahaiyuta loped along the plains to his home. He was met by his people and is now considered a wise man.

Three middle sized baskets lay on the floor. Grandfather was in the kitchen banging about with the pots and pans. He was yelling at the dogs. I stretched and moved to the door. The dogs were chasing each other around with a pair of Grandfather's boxer shorts in the lead dog's mouth.

The widow came outside in her high black boots and a skimpy house dress. "You come back here, Rough-Stuff." The lead dog walked to her with his head down. The widow pulled the boxer shorts out of the dog's mouth, but not without a good rip. She smacked the dog on the nose and he ran off.

"Here, you old man, now you have another hole."

She waved the shorts at Grandfather. "You want some lunch?" Grandfather met her halfway across the yard. "You betcha, what you got cooking?" She smiled and gave him a hug. "You better get that granddaughter of yours. You work her too hard, both her hands and her ears." Grandfather yelled to me. I grabbed my boots, anxious to get out of the stuffy house.

The widow had her best china out on the dining room table. She served sausage with creamed potatoes and little peas. It was a feast and a relaxing time for all of us.

After the meal, Grandfather cleared the table and as we washed the dishes he decided that he had to tell another story.

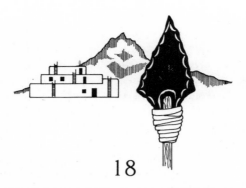

18

THUNDER MOUNTAIN

In a Pueblo, there lived a beautiful woman. This woman, for some reason unknown to me, stayed in her small simple room alone, wanting no one. The roof in her room was made of vigas and crossed cedar which after many years began to wear away, leaving the woman open to the natural elements. Sky Spirit, who was also a lonely spirit, happened to notice this woman living alone, enjoying her own company. Sky Spirit courted and married her, unknown to her people. He came down to her with the dew in the night. She was very happy in his company and enjoyed his visits on a regular basis.

One day she gave birth to a child. The people were very surprised, but kept their feelings to themselves. Her baby boy was stronger than human boys so he grew very fast. His father taught him many magical powers of strength. The boy ran around hunting little animals. His mother's home was filled with feathers and skins from animals. Then he noticed that the men in the village carried strong bows and arrows. He asked his mother to give him a bow and some arrows. She told him that he must get his own just as the other men of the village had done. "Mother, where can I find the wood for bows and arrows?" His mother shuddered to think of the bravery that was needed to get the wood. He asked her over and over again every day and at last, to calm him, she told him of the cliff where there was a great cave and near this cave was the tree which had the wood that makes bows and the bushes that arrows come from. There was so much there that many bows and arrows could be made. "But in the cave is a fierce bear and so no one goes near there. He has already devoured many of our people already." The boy thought that he would not go near there.

The next morning his mother was busy with her work. The boy ran down to the river and crawled along the bank until he could get to the side of the cliff. He climbed up until he came to the place in the rocks on the east side of Thunder Mountain. The opening of the cave was entirely covered with fine wood and oak. Straight sprouts were growing everywhere. "Here is the wood I need," said the boy as he looked at it. "But I don't see any bear, I think I will climb up and see if there is anything in the cave."

He started climbing into the cave. Lightning was sent down by his father and the mouth of the cave closed together. The boy waited and the lightning stopped, the mouth of the cave opened up again. He started to go in, the lightning came down once more to remind him that he should not go into the cave.

He waited and tried again and the fourth time the lightning stopped, his father deciding that the boy must choose his own path. The boy went into the cave. He could not see and he walked into a bear. The bear picked up the boy and squeezed him very tightly.

The boy, in fear of being squeezed to death, squeaked out, "Stop, wait, think of my poor beautiful mother." The bear let his grip loosen and asked, "Is your mother truly beautiful?" The boy quickly spoke, "Yes, my mother is the most beautiful woman in the land." The bear set the boy down and asked him why he had entered his cave. The boy told him. The bear showed the boy how to cut the wood, told him how to carve and dry the wood for a good bow and strong arrows. The bear said that he would let the boy go on one condition, that he could come at sunset and meet the boy's mother and see if the boy had made the bow and arrows correctly. The boy agreed.

The boy ran home. His mother was busy with other things and only noticed that he was home. He went right to work on his bow, carefully stretching it the way the bear had taught him. The boy then took the shorter wood and carved points on the end of each arrow as the bear had told him. Then the boy studied his arrows and felt that they were not as sharp as they could be, so he went to the edge of the plains and gathered up some obsidian rock. This he chipped to sharp points and wrapped tightly to the end of his arrows.

He was still at work when sunset came, he looked up and saw the bear coming. The bear came up to the ladder of his house. The bear asked if he could meet his mother, the boy answered that his mother was very busy but soon she would be home. The bear studied the boy's bow and arrows. The boy showed him the black obsidian arrowheads on the ends. The bear laughed at the boy telling him that the black stones were only coal.

The boy said, "It is hard, it is obsidian."

The bear smiled, "All right, if that is what you believe, but I will prove that the end of your arrow is coal. I will let you shoot me with your weak little black pointed arrows." The boy watched the bear walk to the end of his home and stand up on two legs. The boy aimed and shot the bear. The arrow pierced the bear's heart, killing him dead.

The people heard the loud noise and came running. The mother was amazed to see the dead white bear. The boy explained that the bear had wanted him to try out his arrows and he did. The boy skinned the white bear and hung up the skin to show the Pueblo people that they could now go and gather all the wood that they needed for bows and arrows. That night his mother told him that he would soon become a man.

The widow laughed, "Yes, and then what trouble he can get into. Let's hope that he can keep his underwear away from the dogs." Grandfather stood up, stretched, and started out of the room. "Speaking of dogs, I'd better go check on them." With a bang of the door Grandfather was gone.

The widow rolled out some sopaipilla dough. The grease was spitting in the hot cooker. We had agreed that hot sopaipillas would be great for dinner. She handed me the squares and I turned them in the hot cooker. The pillows puffed up and floated in circles as I tried to spoon them out. The widow smiled, "Did I ever tell you the story about my father?"

"No, but I would like to hear it." She handed me a bigger spoon and started her story.

19

CLIFF OF BIRDS

My father, old man Mandan, told me about a cliff. He had been there twenty or thirty times. When he was twelve years of age, he went there for a dream vision. For two nights he did not dream, brain vision was gone. On the third night a vision of smoke came to him and asked, "Why, why, do you stay here?"

He answered, "I need to find my power."

The smoke vision whispered, "Stay."

Old man Mandan slept on hard ground one more night — when he awoke he was saddened to realize that he had not dreamed nor had visions of any kind. He sat on a large lava stone and wondered what was happening to him. As Sun moved up in the sky he saw drawings on the lava stone he was sitting on, they were under him. Old man Mandan heard a ferocious sound coming from the sky. He held his hand over his eyes to see what was coming at him. Birds flew at him from the clear sky. They flew directly at him as if to hit him or knock him down. They did not touch him, but disappeared into the stone that he was leaning against.

Old man Mandan stayed another night, the fourth night, and dreamed of being a powerful leader and medicine man who at the end of his life would become one with the earth, just as the birds had flying into the rock.

My father was a good hunter, he led his people on many raids, and he had powers to cure the illness in both women and men. On the night before a raiding party, he dreamed of the birds. He told us of the beauty of each bird as clearly as if we were seeing it ourselves. My father was killed in the raiding party.

The young men went many times to the rocks and many times they saw faces on the rocks and knew that those whose faces were on the

111

high rocks, would usually be killed on that raid or hunt. The sides of the cliffs soon were covered with many faces as well as stories. Important stories of battles, births, change of weather or of Pueblos having to move. My father was considered a very wise man. His chants are still sung and his name is remembered although his Pueblo is far to the southeast of here.

Before my father, old man Mandan, went out on a hunt or a raid he would sing us this song:
How is it grandpa that you smile without moving your lips
Your sadness hurts my soul with your words, yet your eyes sparkle
Your hands show fear yet they do not tremble
Your path is steadier than mine yet you are old and fragile
Skeleton ghosts feed on my youth
You have chased them off
Deer carry spirits in their
Horns that look out on us
The spirits know who shall be rewarded
Who not.

The widow rubbed her fingers together. We were both sticky with honey. She smiled at me only allowing the sides of her mouth to lift. "I miss my father, appreciate yours while he is here." We wrapped some sopaipillas up to freeze. The snow blew across the driveway as I thought of my grandfather.

The widow pointed out the window with her long wooden spoon. "Whenever I look out at that blowing snow, I think of Kolowisi." She shuddered returning to the stove to cook.

"Who is Kolowisi?" I asked.

"Oh, let me tell you."

20

KOLOWISI

When I was a little girl, I would go with my aunt to visit family in different Pueblos. On one visit we came to a Pueblo where men were running around the plaza screaming, "Death to the enemy! Death to those who steal our women or our food!" The children ran and hid. The grandfathers carried their grandchildren back out into the plaza on their backs. This one time birds came flying down into the center of the plaza screeching and diving down for the raw meat that was hung on a pole. The men who were dancing grabbed sticks and ran after the grandfathers, hitting the children on their backs and making blood-curdling screams. It was terrifying.

From the back of the Pueblo, a large object came weaving into the plaza. It was Kolowisi. The tremendous serpent opened and closed its mouth, blowing foul breath and seeds from its huge fangs. The children jumped off their grandfathers' backs and grabbed the seeds, hurrying home with as much as they could carry. The seeds were filled with fertility, growth and wisdom. These would be eaten all winter and the seeds that were saved would be planted in the spring for fat, juicy corn. This dance was done to remind the people of the great and wonderful Kolowisi that once came upon the earth to bring life. Kolowisi does not come anymore.

There was an Old Hag who was very poor. She wore dirty torn rags, her hair was matted and falling out, but her hands were very special. The great Kolowisi, the life giving serpent, would come up from under the ground to her, the Old Hag. The earth would tremble, rocks would fall into the underworld, but the people knew that this was good. Kolowisi was coming to them. The Old Hag would carefully walk to Kolowisi and nurse at the large breasts. The milk that came from this magical serpent brought eternal life to those who drank it.

The Old Hag would carefully climb down the ladder to the land of the Dead and she would feed the Kakio, the dead ones. They would gulp down whatever the Old Hag made them without so much as a thank you.

The Old Hag would return to this world with nothing. The people would beg her for some of the great Kolowisi's milk, but she would not give them any. You see, she had made a deal with the Kakio. They would not take any of her children as long as she brought them the milk.

It came to pass that many of the people in this place died from lack of food. The Kakio now had beautiful young women to cook for them. They had young men to order around. They sent the young men down to the underworld to find the path to Kolowisi. The men tunneled, leading the beautiful young maidens with them to the sacred place of Kolowisi. Kolowisi liked the gentle touch of the young maidens. the Old Hag was no longer needed.

The poeple chanted and prayed hoping that Kolowisi would return to the surface and give them life. Kolowisi never returned. The ground rarely shakes here anymore and the Old Hag wanders around the hills in the snow calling Kolowisi. The Kakio took her children, but they don't want her, she's too old, too ugly, and they have no use for her. Some say she comes to the house when a child is going to die. She tries to call the Kolowisi through the dying child, but it doesn't work, at least not yet.

The wind continued to blow against the house. The dogs barked, chasing each other around in the blowing snow.

GLOSSARY

A'age — sweet atole dance
Agoyo P'in — Star Mountain
Agoyo Ovin — many star mountain
Anina — old wise woods
Ba'a Ta — striped woven belt
Bubinge — plaza
Buta'a — circle dance
Cacique — census taker
Hegeih T'a — marked runoff, arroyo
Huu Ts'say — yellow cedar bark
Gwingweni-e — standing dance
Janini-povi — ?wandering flower?
Kaa Pee Tsawa — birth of green leaves
Kaiye — mother's older sister
Kay-Sen D'oh — great white bear
Kaye' — fetish stone
Kha Povi — rose flower
Khaayay P'oekwin — sacred rock lake
Khan P'in — Lion Mountain
Khan Ts'ay — yellow lion
Khuu Kaay — corn leaf
Khuu Kwa'a'aa-i — corn beads
Khowa Ts'say — yellow husk
Khunjo' — wolf
Ki'i — father's sister
Ko'o — mother's younger sister
Kudioaniyima — two corn ears ceremony
Kukayee — kernelled ears of corn
Kuliohatsiper — corn blowing ceremony
Kuriohatsipe — two ears of corn by infant
Kuu Oyegi — corn frost

Kwahtaa — thunder roar
Munu — agitation, unrest
Muuyo Sen Ts'aa — white horned shell man
Mwe'e — scraping music stick
Nan Povi — shining aspen flower
Naposhun — sacred black clay
Nee-nee — butterfly
Nuukhun — dark
O'e — ceremony
Oekuu Tsaa — small white turtle
Oga — cowrie shell
Ouuwah — mask
Oxua — cloud, rain spirit
Oyegei Thim'uu — sparkling frost flakes
P'aa Sen — buck deer
Paayogedi — summer, warm season
Pawha — dragging fish
Pensendo — Deer Spirit Elder
P'in P'oe — journey
Pingxeng — game priest
Povi — flower
Pu'fona — delivering baby doctor (midwife)
Sawipinge — main singer
Semixua — male mask paint
Sibo'pene — overflowing kiva or Pueblo
Soekhuwa-Ts'aa — white fog
Tambe — drum
Tambefe — drumstick
Tenyo — stalk seeker
Than Bee — turning sun
Thu Ts'aa — white clay
Tinini — shell fragile frame
To'e — antelope
Tsabi 'yu — boogie man
Tsay-Whan T'a — marked eagle tail
T'see — magic black stone, obsidian
Tsiowenu Ku — lightning stone, arrow or spear point
Tsitsayiya — navel mother names infant
Tsi Owena Ku — lightning stone
Tssawa — dark blue or green lights
Woe Sedo' — Old Man Medicine

Yoe Tsideh — cactus bird
Yugeh — calm, peace

Translations are the author's personal interpretations.